READWELL'S

ARABIC FOR

IN A M

Easy Method of Learning Arabic
Through English Without a Teacher

Mrs. Rekha Chawla
B.A. (Cairo)

Readwell Publications
NEW DELHI-110008

Published by :
READWELL PUBLICATIONS
B-8, Rattan Jyoti, 18, Rajendra Place
New Delhi-110 008 (INDIA)
Phone : 25737448, 25712649, 25721761
Fax : 91-11-25812385
E-mail : readwell@sify.com
newlight@vsnl.net

ISBN 81-87782-20-X

Printed at : Arya Offset Press, New Delhi.

PREFACE

At a time when there is a great rush of Indians to the Arab countries in view of better employment opportunities there, it has become essential to have a working knowledge of the Arabic language for those who are going there. This facilitates living among the Arabs and makes their day-to-day life easy.

In view of this need, we have pleasure in bringing out a book on the teaching of the Arabic language through the media of English and Hindi. We have divided the whole book in many parts and have given a few lessons in basic grammar. The difficulty with the Arabic language is that it is spoken and written differently in different Arab countries. Sometimes the difference is so great that a person from one Arab country cannot understand the Arabic spoken in another Arab country. We have, therefore, tried to teach in such a way that the learner will feel at home in any Arab country, even though he may not be completely conversant with the language of the area in which he is living. We have added a few pages of vocabulary also to facilitate a working knowledge of the essential parts of the language. We have every hope that the learners will be happy with this small work. We shall always be happy to receive any constructive suggestion for improving this work still further.

Authors

Contents

Alphabets

ARABIC ALPHABET عربي حروف ابجد	PRONUNCIATION تلفظ	GNG ALPH. CORRESP. ARABIC متبادل حروف	ARABIC ALPHABET عربي حروف ابجد	PRONUNCIATION تلفظ	ENG ALPH. CORRESP. ARABIC متبادل حروف
أ ا	Alef	a	صـ ص ـص	Ssad	ss
بـ ب ـب	Ba	b	ضـ ض ـض	Dad	dh
تـ ت ـت	ta	t	ط ـط	Tah	t
ثـ ث ـث	Tha	th	ظ ـظ	Zah	z
جـ ج ـج	Jeem	j	عـ ع ـع	Ein	ei
حـ ح ـح	Ha	h	غـ غ ـغ	Ghein	gh
خـ خ ـخ	Kha	kh	فـ ف ـف	Fa	f
د ـد	Dal	d	قـ ق ـق	Quaf	q
ذ ـذ	Thal	th	كـ ك ـك	Kat	k
ر ـر	Ra	r	لـ ل ـل	Lam	l
ز ـز	Zein	z	مـ م ـم	Meem	m
سـ س ـس	Seen	c,s	نـ ن ـن	Noon	n
شـ ش ـش	Sheen	sh	هـ ـه	Ha	h
			و ـو	Wao	w
			يـ ي	Ya	y

Vowels

a	as 'a' in alcohol	ee	(long 'i') as 'ea' in beast
aa	(long) as 'a' in art	u	as ''oo' in foot
i	as 'i' in sin	oo	(long 'u') as 'oo' in food

Consonants

b	as in bag	r	as in ring
f	as in fat	s	as in set
j	as in jar	z	as in zest
k	as in kettle	sh	as in ship
l	as in let	d	as 'th' in this
m	as in mother	t	as 'th' in seventh
n	as in night	kh	as 'ch' in Munich

Dipthongs

ai	as 'i' in night	aw	as 'ou' in shout

Writing runs from right to left and the letters consist of strokes or strokes and dots. Vowels are not counted letters. There are two classes of letters; those which can be joined on both sides and those which can only be joined to the preceding letter. The first class has four forms, initial, medial, final, and independent; the second has two, final and independent. The essential part of the letter remains unchanged as is shown here :—

independent	final	medial	initial
ب	ـب	ـبـ	بـ

when there is a final flourish the dot or dots are often put in the middle of it.

Name.	Independent.	Final.	Medial.	Initial.	Equivalent.
alif	ا	ـا			ʾ
bā	ب	ـب	ـبـ	بـ	b
tā	ت	ـت	ـتـ	تـ	t
thā	ث	ـث	ـثـ	ثـ	θ
jīm	ج	ـج	ـجـ	جـ	j

Name.	Independent.	Final.	Medial.	Initial.	Equivalent.
ḥā	ح	ـح	ـحـ	حـ	ħ
khā	خ	ـخ	ـخـ	خـ	x
dāl	د	ـد			d
dhāl	ذ	ـذ			ð
rā	ر	ـر			r
zā	ز	ـز			z
sīn	س	ـس	ـسـ	سـ	s
shīn	ش	ـش	ـشـ	شـ	ʃ
ṣād	ص	ـص	ـصـ	صـ	ṣ
ḍād	ض	ـض	ـضـ	ضـ	ḍ
ṭā	ط	ـط	ـطـ	طـ	ṭ
ẓā	ظ	ـظ	ـظـ	ظـ	ð̣
'ain	ع	ـع	ـعـ	عـ	ʕ
ghain	غ	ـغ	ـغـ	غـ	ɣ
fā	ف	ـف	ـفـ	فـ	f
ḳāf	ق	ـق	ـقـ	قـ	q
kāf	ك	ـك	ـكـ	كـ	k
lām	ل	ـل	ـلـ	لـ	l
mīm	م	ـم	ـمـ	مـ	m
nūn	ن	ـن	ـنـ	نـ	n
hā	ه	ـه	ـهـ	هـ	h
waw	و	ـو			w
yā	ى	ـى	ـيـ	يـ	y

The Arabic alphabet consists of twenty-eight letters. Some of these letters have no equivalents in the English

VOWELS

ا	آ	اِ	اِى	اُ	اُو	اَى	اَو
a	aa	i	ee	u	oo	ay	aw

Three, which occur both short and long, are recognised in writing. Doubtless there were many variations in speech but only one is mentioned here. The consonants *alif*, 'w,' and 'y' were used to indicate the long 'a', 'u', and 'i'. The signs are put above or below the consonant which precedes the vowel.

NAME.	SIGN.	SOUND.	SYMBOL.
i, short	ـِ	as in 'sin'	*i*
long	ـِي	as in 'yeast'	*i:*
u, short	ـُ	much as in south English 'foot'	*u*
long	ـُو	much as in 'food' . . .	*u:*
a, short	ـَ	as in south English 'bat' .	*a*
long	ـَا	as in south English 'man' (drawled)	*a:*

There are two diphthongs:

ai	ـَي	much as in south English 'fight'	*ay*
au	ـَو	much as in south English 'shout'	*aw*

Near an emphatic consonant 'a' short is like the vowel in 'not', 'a' long is like that in 'was' (drawled); represented by *v* and *v:*; and *ay* becomes more like the sound in 'boy'. There is no English equivalent of *aw* under these circumstances; the 'a' component becomes *v*.

CONSONANTS

ا	ب	ت	ث	ج	ح	خ	د
a-aa	b	ṭ	ṭ(s)	j	ḥ	ḳh	ḍ
ذ	ر	ز	س	ش	ص	ض	ط
ḍ(z)	r	z	s	sh	s	ḍ	ṭ
ظ	ع	غ	ف	ق	ك	ل	م
ẓ	'a	gh	f	q	k	l	m
		ن	ه	و	ى		
		n	h	w	y.		

In writing it is often convenient to put one consonant above another :— بح *bħ* ; لمح *lmħ* ; لجم *ljm* ; حجج *ħjj*.

Twelve of the consonants form correlative pairs.

	Tip of Tongue				Back of tongue towards soft palate	Throat and larynx
	Between teeth	Touching upper teeth	Behind lower teeth (see below)	Behind upper teeth		
Breathed unsingable .	θ	t	ŧ	s	x	ħ
Voiced singable .	ð	d	đ	z	ɣ	ʕ

The rest, including liquids and semivowels, stand in the next table in the order of their articulation, beginning with the lips and ending with the glottis, i.e. the space between the vocal cords, which may close the glottis completely in a stop ʔ or remain apart allowing the passage of breath in *h*.

	Labial	Labio-dental	Dental	Gums	Palatal	Velar	Uvular	Glottal
Voiced .	b		ð		j	ɣ		h
Breathed .		f		ʃ s		k	q	ʔ (h)
Liquids and semi vowels (voiced)	m w		l	r n	y			

The six pairs :—

θ as English 'th' in 'think'.
ð as 'th' in 'this'.
ṭ as 't' in 'eighth'.
ḍ as 'd' in 'width'.
ŧ voiceless, đ voiced ; counterparts of 't' and 'd'.

SUN LETTERS

التّاجر تاجر ت
ṭ ṭaajir trader aṭṭaajir

الذئب ذئب ذ
z ziab wolf azziab

الثّمن ثمن ث
ṭ ṭaman value aṭṭaman

الرّيح ريح ر
r reeḥ wind arreeḥ

الدّم دم د
ḍ ḍam blood aḍḍam

الزّبدة زبدة ز
z zubda butter azzubdaa

السّوق سوق س
s sooq bazaar assooq

الطّريق طريق ط
ṭ ṭareeq road aṭṭareeq

الشّك شك ش
sh shak doubt ashshak

الظّرف ظرف ظ
ẓ ẓarf vessel aẓẓarf

الصّوت صوت ص
s sawṭ sound assawṭ

اللّبن لبن ل
l laban curd allaban

الضّرب ضرب ض
ḍ ḍarb beating aḍḍarb

النّهر نهر ن
n nahr river annahr

ا	أب		الأب	ف	فم		الفم
a	ab	father	alab	t	fam	mouth	alfam
ب	بنت		البنت	ق	قلب		القلب
b	binṭ	girl	albint	q	qalb	heart	alqalb
ج	جمل		الجمل	ك	كلب		الكلب
j	jamal	camel	aljamal	k	kalb	dog	alkalb
ح	حل		الحل	م	مطر		المطر
h	ḥal	solution	alḥal	m	maṭar	rain	almaṭar
خ	خبر		الخبر	ه	هندى		الهندى
ḳh	ḳhabar	news	alḳhabar	h	hinḍee	Indian	alhinḍee
ع	عم		العم	و	ورق		الورق
’a	am	uncle	al’am	w	waraq	leaf	alwaraq
غ	غلام		شغل	ى	يد		جيش
gh	ghulaam	boy	shaghl	y	yaḍ	hand	jaysh

Emphatics.—Tip of tongue behind lower teeth, blade behind upper teeth touching gums. There is a depression or hollowing of the tongue just behind this and a raising of the back of the tongue. The sides of the tongue make a sort of inverted lid for the upper jaw, overflowing the back teeth and just touching the inside of the cheeks. The back of the tongue is raised in the same way for the other two emphatics ṣ and ð.

s breathed, **z** voiced.

s is a strong clear sound as in ‘hissing’ to be sharply differentiated from the emphatic ṣ; the tip of the tongue is behind the upper teeth.

z is a clear buzzing sound as in whizzing.

x breathed, **ɣ** voiced.

x is like the ‘ch’ in the Scottish ‘loch’ or the German ‘ach’ but more scrapy. The difficulty is not so much in the sound as in the positions in which it can occur

—e.g. initially. Pronounce 'loch' and then try to pronounce it backwards.

ɣ bears a similar relation to **x** as **z** does to **s**. Try to voice **x**, that is, make it a singable sound, put the buzz of voice into it. Make it a little further back than **x**; do not roll it, thus making it a back **r**.

ħ breathed, **ʕ** voiced.

ħ differs from **h**, which is frequently voiced, and has a sharper friction of an entirely different resonance caused by the forced depression of the back of the tongue and the tightening of the throat, the larynx being raised at the same time. The back of the tongue is as low as when the doctor presses it down with a spoon. With **a** it is very like the stage whisper 'ha!' It must not be produced with scrapy friction which confuses it with **x**.

ʕ is the voiced correlative of **ħ** pronounced with more tightening of the throat and forcing up of the larynx. The feeling in the throat is suggestive of slight retching. If you pronounce English vowels with a tightened throat and squeezed larynx, producing a metallic, rather low-pitched voice, they will be near to Arabic vowels in the neighbourhood of this consonant.

The two remaining emphatics:—

ṣ is the counterpart of **s** and is made with the blade of the tongue against the teeth ridge, the tip being behind the lower teeth.

ð̣ is the counterpart of **ð**; it is interdental but the tip of the tongue points upwards to the upper lip.

The four emphatics and **q** give to the vowel 'a', when it precedes or follows them, special dark qualities like the vowel in 'not'.

q is the furthest back **k** sound you can make, with the back of the tongue closing the arches of the back of the mouth, which are laterally squeezed nearer together to make the closure easier.

ʃ as in 'ship'. In Arabic **s** and **h** can come together without producing the **ʃ** sound.

ʔ the glottal stop. This sound is commonly used in Cockney instead of 't' in words like 'better'.

'bottle' and also in standard English when a wo
which begins with a vowel is strongly emphasized,
ʔ absolutely ʔ awful.

r is rolled as in Scotland; never fricative as in southern England.

The other consonants need no remark.

OTHER CONVENTIONAL SIGNS

Madda.—This takes the place of hamza when *aː* follows the glottal stop. This sound group may be original or it may be derived from the group *ʔaʔ*, which to Arabs is unpronounceable. In both cases it is written آ. So آكَلَ *ʔaːkala* may stand for *ʔaːkala* 'he ate with' and *ʔaʔkala* 'he fed' (transitive).

Sukûn.—Every consonant, which has no vowel immediately following it, is marked by sukûn ْ. This of course does not apply when the consonant is a letter of prolongation, only indicates a long vowel, as in سُو *suː*, contrasted with سَوْ *saw*, or when it is written but not pronounced, as اَلدّارُ *addaːru*, where the 'l' is assimilated to the 'd'.

Liaison.—Some words should begin with two consonants. From what has been said about the syllable it is clear that this is impossible so a helping vowel is put before the first consonant when the word stands alone. This vowel is indicated by *alif* always. If such a word stands alone the helping vowel is ushered in by the glottal stop. In connected speech the helping vowel is dropped and the final vowel of the preceding word takes its place. If there is no final vowel, a short one, usually 'i', is inserted.

In connected speech the sign ʼ is written over the *alif*.

In liaison a final long vowel is shortened in pronunciation and a diphthong is resolved into its component parts.

The best manner is never to write hamza over the liaison *alif*

Hamza.—This is the glottal stop
The sign ٔ is usually written with one of the three consonants *alif*, *w*, or *y*, which is called its bearer. *y*, when written with hamza, always loses its dots.

Hamza always has *alif* at the beginning of a word and, after the vowel 'a', at the end.

After a long vowel it has no bearer except in the sequence *a:ʔi* when it usually has 'y'.

After sukûn it may be written over a line connecting two letters.

أَقْرَأُ *ʔaqraʔu* ; إِبِلٌ *ʔibilun* ; أُذُنٌ *ʔudunun*

كِسَاءٌ *kisa:ʔun* ; سَاءَلَ *sa:ʔala* ; مَسْـُٔولٌ *masʔu:lun*

أَبْنَائِهِ *ʔabna:ʔihi* ; سُؤَالٌ *suʔa:lun* ; أَسْئِلَةٌ *ʔasʔilatun*

To find out how to write hamza.—Pronounce the word as if the hamza were not there, write the result, and add hamza. Take the word *fuʔa:dun*. Without hamza it becomes *fuwa:dun*, which is the correct way to write it, فُوَادٌ then add hamza فُؤَادٌ. The plural of this word is *ʔafʔidatun*; without hamza it becomes *ʔafi:datun*. This is أَفِيدَةٌ remove the dots from the 'y' and add hamza, and remove 'i' one step to the left, أَفْئِدَةٌ is the right spelling.

Nunation.—The word nunation is formed from the Arabic name of the letter 'n'. In one class of nouns the final vowel, which is the case ending, is written twice to indicate the pronunciations *un*, *an*, *in* respectively. With 'u' the upper sign is usually reversed ٌ or ٌ is used instead.

مَدِينَةٌ *madi:natun* ; مَدِينَةً *madi:natan* ; مَدِينَةٍ *madi:natin*.

Shadda.—If the same consonant is repeated and no vowel comes between the two, it is written once and the sign shadda ّ put over it. This may be due to assimilation, as in *adda:ru* above, or it may be part of the word form; thus كَسَرَ *kasara*, 'he broke,' but كَسَّرَ *kassara*, 'he smashed,' when the first syllable ends with 's' and the second begins with 's'. Apparent exceptions are due to the fact that the two consonants belong to different words as اَللَّيْلُ *allaylu.* The first 'l' belongs to the article and the second to the noun. The first 'l' does not take sukûn because it has been assimilated to the second and is indicated by shadda.

Syllable.—Every syllable must begin with one consonant; the glottal stop is a consonant. A syllable may consist of consonant and vowel or of consonant vowel consonant.

ACCENT

The accent rests on—

(1) The penultimate syllable when it is long; i.e. has a long vowel or two consonants. *ki'ta:bun, ya'ku:nu.*

(2) On the antepenultimate when it is long and the penultimate short; when a word has three short syllables. *'ka:tibun, 'kataba.*

(3) On the long syllable before the antepenultimate when the penultimate and the antepenultimate are both short *mu'ka:tabatun*; on the first syllable if there is no such long vowel *'katabatuhuma:.*

Note that monosyllables and the definite article which are joined in writing to the following word do not affect the accent.

wa-'kataba; al-'madadu

The words

اِبْتِدَاءِ *ibtida:ʔi* اِنْهِزَامِ *inhiza:mi* اَلْعَدُوِّ *alʕaduwwi*

when connected, read

فِي ٱبْتِدَاءِ ٱنْهِزَامِ ٱلْعَدُوِّ

fibtida:ʔinhiza:milʕaduwwi (note that *fi:* is shortened).

يَدَىْ *yaday* becomes *yadayi*

يَدَيِ ٱلْكَلْبِ *yadayilkalbi*

رَمَوْا *ramaw* (*alif* is purely graphic) becomes *ramawu*

رَمَوُا ٱلْعَدُوَّ *ramawulʕaduwwa*

The Arabs call this هَمْزَةُ ٱلْوَصْلِ ***hamzatulwasli.***

اسم کی قسمیں

Noun

انواع الأسم

Nouns are of two kinds: | اسم کی دو قسمیں ہیں | يقسم الاسم الى نوعين :

1. *Proper Noun* | (۱) اسم معرفہ | ١ – اسم علم

2. *Common Noun* | (۲) اسم نکرہ | ٢ – اسم نكرة

– اما اسم العلم فانه يدل على شخص او حيوان او مكان معين :

کسی خصوصی جگہ، انسان یا حیوان کے نام کو اسم معرفہ کہا جاتا ہے

مثلاً :

Example:

Ahmed *George* *Diana*	*Names of persons*	اشخاص کے نام	احمد جورج ديانا
Boby *Farhood* *Rantantan*	*Names of animals*	حیوانوں کے نام	بوبي فرهود رنتانتان
Beirut *London* *Cairo*	*Names of places*	جگہوں کے نام	بيروت لندن القاهرة

Adhameer

الضمير

ضمیر

The pronoun

أ – الضمير كلمة تقوم مقام الاسم :

Adhameer kalimat taqoum maqam al ism.

ضمیر وہ لفظ ہے جو اسم کی جگہ استعمال ہوتا ہے

The pronoun is a word that takes the place of a noun.

Example:	مثلاً	Mathalan	مثلاً :
I	میں	Ana	انا
you	تم	Anta, Anti	انتَ ، انتِ
He	وہ (مذکر)	Hoa	هو
She	وہ (موئنث)	Hia	هي
it	یہ	Hoa, Hia lighair El Akél.	هو او هي لغير العاقل
we	ہم	Nahnou	نحن
you	تم (جمع)	Antom, Antonna	انتم ، انتن
they	وہ (جمع)	Hom, Honna	هم ، هن

These are the personal pronouns :

ضمائر شخصیہ یہ ہیں

هذه هي الضمائر الشخصية :

Hathihihia adhamair ashakhsiat

The demonstrative pronouns

ضمائر اشارہ

ب – ضمائر الاشارة

Singular, Masculine and Feminine

واحد ، مذکر و موئنث

Near : This	یہ (قریب)	Hatha	هذا	Lilkareeb :	للقريب :
Far : That	وہ (دور)	Thaka	ذاك	Lilbaiid	للبعيد :

Plural Masculine and Feminine

الجمع المذكر والمؤنث

Near:	قریب These	یہ (جمع)	Hàola	هؤلاء : lilkareeb	للقريب

The possessive pronouns or adjectives »

د – ضمائر الملكية او الاضافة

Dhamair el malalkiat au al idhafat.

الضمائر التي تستعمل صفات للتملك
وهي الضمائر المتصلة في اللغة العربية

Possessive adjectives are used before nouns

My book	میری کتاب	Kitabi	كتابي
Your book	تمہاری کتاب	Kitaboka	كتابكَ
His book	اس (مذکر) کی کتاب	Kitaboho	كتابهُ
Her book	اس (مونث) کی کتاب	Kitaboha	كتابها
Its head	اس کا سر	Rasoha	رأسها
Our pens	ہمارے قلم	Aklamona	اقلامنا
Your hats	تمہاری ٹوپیاں	Baraneetkom	برانيطكم
Their cars	ان کی کاریں	Sayyaratohom	سياراتهم

Personal pronouns with verb «Have»

١٤ـ استعمال الضمائر مع فعل التملك
ويعبر عنها في العربية ب عندي
وعندك وعنده الخ ...

I have	میں رکھتا ہوں	**Indy**	عندي
You have	تم رکھتے ہو	**Indak**	عندك
He has	وہ رکھتا ہے	**Indaho**	عنده
She has	وہ رکھتی ہے	**Indaha**	عندها
It has	یہ رکھتا ہے	**Indaha au Indaho**	عندها او عنده لغير العاقل
We have	ہم رکھتے ہیں	**Indana**	عندنا
You have	تم (جمع) رکھتے ہو	**Indakom**	عندكم
They have	وہ رکھتے ہیں	**Indahom**	عندهم او عندهن

Personal pronouns with verb «to see»			١٥ – الضمائر مع فعل «يرى»
I see you	میں تمہیں دیکھتا ہوں	Ana arak	انا اراك
You see me	تم مجھے دیکھتے ہو	Anta tarani	انت تراني
He sees her	وہ اسے (مونث) دیکھتا ہے	Howa yaraha	هو براها
She sees him	وہ اسے (مذکر) دیکھتی ہے	Hiya taraho	هي تراهُ
We see you	ہم تمہیں دیکھتے ہیں	Nahno Narakom	نحن نراكم
You see us	تم ہمیں دیکھتے ہو	Antom tarawna	انتم ترونا
They see us	وہ ہمیں دیکھتے ہیں	Hom yarauna	هم يروننا
		au honna yarauna	او هن يروننا

NOUN AND ARTICLES

The distinction between a definite and an indefinite noun is fundamental.

The indefinite article *n* is put at the end of the noun, is not expressed by a consonant, but is indicated in one class of nouns by nunation. For inflection the noun falls into four classes but, as two of them are indeclinable, they cannot be called declensions. This lesson deals with one class only.

نَهْرٌ *nahrun* a river ; مَلِكٌ *malikun* a king

The *u* is the nominative inflection.

One way of making a noun definite is to give it the definite article اَلْ *al*, which is written in front of the noun and joined to it. The vowel of the article is only a helping vowel, liaison, so in connected speech it is replaced by the final vowel of the preceding word. If the noun begins with a dental, sibilant, *r*, *l*, or *n*

ن ل ظ ط ض ص ش س ز ر ذ د ث ت

that letter assimilates to itself the *l* of the article in pronunciation though the *l* is still written. The assimilating consonant takes *shadda.* No noun can be both definite and indefinite at the same time, so nunation must be dropped when the definite article is present. اَلْبَيْتُ *albaytu* the house ; اَلشَّمْسُ *aʃʃamsu* the sun. Arabic uses the definite article where English does not ; abstract nouns usually have it ; and it also indicates the class. ' Man is a reasoning animal ' must be translated ' The man '.

An adjective, which qualifies a noun, follows it, agrees with it in gender (if it is singular), in case, and in definiteness.

بُسْتَانٌ كَبِيرٌ *busta:nun kabi:run* a big garden.

اَلْبَحْرُ الْوَاسِعُ *albaħrulwa:siʕu* the spacious sea.

The verbs ' is ' and ' are ' are not expressed ; so ' the man is handsome ' is literally ' the man handsome '. Arabic grammar took its technical terms from logic, so ' the man ' is subject and ' handsome ' (the complement of the verb to be, as we call it) is the predicate. The subject must be definite, unless the sentence is negative or interrogative, and the predicate must be indefinite.

اَلرَّجُلُ حَسَنٌ *arrajulu ħasanun* the man is handsome.

اَلْبَحْرُ وَاسِعٌ *albaħru wa:siʕun* the sea is spacious.

Questions are asked by prefixing one of the particles أ *ʔa* or هَلْ *hal* to the sentence ; *ʔa* is connected with the word it precedes.

أَرَجُلٌ *ʔarajulun* . . . is a man . . . ?

Three nouns are half way to having three radicals :—

أَبٌ (آبَاءٌ) 'father': أَخٌ (إِخْوَةٌ—إِخْوَانٌ)

'brother': حَمٌ (أَحْمَاءٌ) 'husband's father'.

There is nothing peculiar about them when they have one of the articles :—

: اَلْأَخَ — اَلْأَخِ — اَلْأَخُ — أَبًا — أَبٍ — أَبٌ

Of course these forms are rare.

In the construct state the final vowel is lengthened :

أَبَا — أَبِى — أَبُو

and the dual is أَبَوَانِ 'two parents' أَبَوَيْنِ.

The pronominal suffixes are added to the construct state :—

أَبُوكَ 'your father' (nom.) أَبَاهُ 'his father' (acc.)

أَبِيهِ 'his father' (gen.) but : أَبِى 'my father' (all cases)

أَبُو الْمُلُوكِ 'the father of kings' : أَبُو زَيْدٍ 'Zayd's father'.

When a man has a son, he is known not by his own name but as the father of his son.

ذُو 'possessor of' occurs only in the construct state :—

	Sing. Masc.	Sing. Fem.	Dual Masc.	Dual Fem.	Plural Masc.		Plural Fem.
nom.	ذُو	ذَاتُ	ذَوَا	ذَوَاتَا	ذَوُو	أُولُو	ذَوَاتُ

acc. ذَاتَ ذَا
gen. ذَاتِ ذِى } ذَوَاتِ أُولِى ذَوِى ذَوَاتَىْ ذَوَىْ

ذُو is never used with suffixes : it often takes the place of an adjective :—

ذُو عِلْمٍ 'learned', 'a learned man'.

ذُو عَقْلٍ 'intelligent' : ذَاتُ مَالٍ 'rich', 'a rich woman'.

سَنَةٌ 'year' has two plurals سَنَوَاتٌ and سِنُونَ ; the oblique case of the latter is سِنِينَ with assimilation.

فَمٌ 'mouth' is regular but in the construct فُو—فَا—فِى may also be used ; with suffixes : فُوهُ—فَاهُ—فِيهِ but فِىَّ 'my mouth' (all cases).

A few nouns begin with liaison :—

اِبْنٌ (أَبْنَاءٌ) 'son' : اِبْنَةٌ (بَنَاتٌ) 'daughter' : اِسْمٌ : 'two' اِثْنَانِ (masc.) 'two' : اِثْنَتَانِ (fem.) 'two' : اِسْمٌ (أَسْمَاءٌ) 'name' : اِمْرَأَةٌ (نِسَاءٌ—نِسْوَةٌ) 'woman' : اِمْرُؤٌ 'man' اِمْرَءًا (acc.) اِمْرِئٍ (gen.).

إِمْرُؤٌ and إِمْرَأَةٌ drop the liaison after the definite article and become اَلْمَرْءُ and اَلْمَرْأَةُ ; the other nouns keep the liaison : اَلاِبْنُ — اَلاِبْنَةُ .

اِبْنٌ has a sound plural بَنُونَ — بَنِينَ which is used in the names of tribes : بَنُو بَكْرٍ 'the tribe Bakr'.

Note the following spellings :—

بِسْمِ اللّٰهِ 'in the name of God'.

زَيْدُ بْنُ مُحَمَّدٍ *Zaydubnu muhammadin*
Zayd, the son of Muhammad.

زَيْدٌ اُبْنُ مُحَمَّدٍ *Zaydunibnu muhammadin*
Zayd is the son of Muhammad.

In the last example the connecting vowel *i* is not indicated in writing even in vocalized texts.

كِلَا ; fem. كِلْتَا 'both' is used only in the construct state. With a suffix it is inflected for case like any dual, with a noun it is not.

PRONOUN

Demonstrative Pronoun

The letters *ð, h, l, k* have demonstrative force, the pronouns are compounded from them. We have already met *l* in the definite article and the emphatic *la*.

This. The simplest pronoun is *ða:* but more common is the compound *ha:ða:* which is usually written هٰذَا or هَذَا.

	Singular.	Dual.	Plural.
masc.	هٰذَا	هٰذَانِ هٰذَيْنِ	هٰ أُولَاءِ *ha:ʔula:ʔi*
fem.	هٰذِى . هٰذِهِ	هٰتَانِ هٰتَيْنِ	

The inflections of ذَا can be found by cutting off the prefix *ha:*.

That.

	Singular.	Dual.	Plural.
masc.	ذَاكَ	ذَانِكَ ذَيْنِكَ	أُولَائِكَ *ʔula:ʔika*
fem.	تَاكَ تِيكَ	تَانِكَ تَيْنِكَ	

More common in the singular are ذٰلِكَ (masc.) تِلْكَ (fem.).

A demonstrative pronoun precedes its noun and, as it is by nature definite, the noun must be definite also.

هٰذَا الرَّسُولُ this messenger; هٰذِهِ الدَّابَّةُ this riding beast.

But if the noun has a pronominal suffix, the demonstrative follows it.

هٰذَا قُوتُكَ this your food = this food of yours.

If the noun is indefinite you have a sentence :—

هٰذَا قَلَمٌ this is a (reed) pen ; تِلْكَ أَمَةٌ that is a slave girl.

When the predicate of a sentence is definite, the pronoun of the third person is put between the demonstrative and the predicate.

ذٰلِكَ هُوَ ٱلْحَكِيمُ

that is the doctor (literally, wise man).

هٰذِهِ هِيَ ٱلضَّيْعَةُ this is the village (estate).

أُولَائِكَ هُمْ أَصْحَابُ ٱلْحُكُومَةِ

those are the members of the government.

In sentences like these, the demonstrative is a nominative absolute and the real sentence is the personal pronoun plus the predicate. It is a mistake to say that the personal pronoun takes the place of the copula 'is', 'are'.

Interrogative pronouns.

مَنْ 'who ?' مَا 'what ?' These are indeclinable.

مَا when combined with the preposition لِ is often abbreviated لِمَا or لِمَ.

مَنِ ٱلْوَكِيل who is the agent ?

مَنْ صَرَخَ who shouted for help ?

مَنْ ذَكَرْتَ whom did you mention ?

لِمَنِ ٱلْجَوْهَرُ whose is the jewel?

لِمَ نَظَرْتَ إِلَيْهَا for what (why) did you look at her?

مَنْ and مَا are also used as indefinite pronouns and then they behave like conditional particles.

أَيٌّ أَيَّةٌ 'which of' is always followed by a genitive or a pronominal suffix.

أَيُّكُمْ صَعِدَ فِي رَأْسِ ٱلْمَنَارَةِ

which of you went up to the top of the minaret?

RELATIVE CLAUSES

There is no relative pronoun in Arabic.

When the antecedent is indefinite, the relative clause is added without any connecting link.

أَطْلُبُ رَجُلًا يَقُومُ عَلَى بُسْتَانِي

I am looking for a man who will stand over (look after) my garden.

When the antecedent is definite, اَلَّذِي is used as a link between the antecedent and the relative clause. It is inflected as follows:—

	sing.	dual, nom.	oblique	plural
masc.	اَلَّذِي	اَللَّذَانِ	اَللَّذَيْنِ	اَلَّذِينَ
fem.	اَلَّتِي	اَللَّتَانِ	اَللَّتَيْنِ	اَللَّوَاتِي

The link agrees in case with the antecedent; this is visible only in the dual.

When the English relative is in an oblique case, the link has to be supplemented by a personal pronoun in the relative clause. This pronoun is often omitted when it should be in the accusative.

اَلرَّجُلُ ٱلَّذِى قَتَلَ أَبِى

the man who killed my father.

اَلرَّجُلُ ٱلَّذِى قَتَلَهُ أَبِى

the man whom my father killed.

اَلْمَرْأَةُ ٱلَّتِى كَانَ عِنْدَهَا ٱبْنِى

the woman with whom my son was.

أَبْعَثُ إِلَيْكَ ٱلْمَرْأَتَيْنِ ٱلَّتَيْنِ تَطْلُبُ مِنْهُمَا خَبَرَ ٱبْنَتِكَ

I am sending to you the two women from whom you can ask news of your daughter.

If the antecedent is first or second person, the pronoun in the relative clause may agree with it or be in the third person to agree with the link.

أَأَنْتِ ٱلَّتِى ٱسْتَوْدَعْتُكِ ٱلسِّرَّ

are you she to whom I entrusted the secret?

كُنْ أَنْتَ ٱلَّذِى تُكَلِّمُهَا

be you he who speaks to her.

نَحْنُ ٱلَّذِينَ بَايَعُوا مُحَمَّدًا

we are those who did homage to Muḥammad.

'He who' is rendered by الذى or مَنْ ; 'that which' by الذى or مَا.

من may take the verb in the singular or plural ; ما always has a singular verb.

مَنْ أَشْعَرُ الْعَرَبِ قَالَ اَلَّذِى يَقُولُ....

who is the most poetical of the Arabs? he said, he who says....

يَا مَنْ لَا يَمُوتُ اِرْحَمْ

O, he who dies not, have mercy = you who die not have mercy.

عَرَفْتُ مَا عَرَفْتَهُ

I know what you know.

أَىٌّ 'which of' is always followed by a genitive, either a noun or a pronominal suffix. It may be singular or plural and may belong to the main sentence or the relative clause.

سَلِّمْ عَلَى أَيُّهُمْ أَفْضَلُ

or

سَلِّمْ عَلَى أَيِّهِمْ أَفْضَلُ

greet those (him) of them who are most worthy.

The commonest forms for the plural of short nouns are :—

أَفْعُلٌ — فُعُلٌ — فِعَالٌ — فُعُولٌ — أَفْعَالٌ

For some forms of the plural rules can be given.

أَفْعِلَاءُ is a plural of فَعِيلٌ : صَدِيقٌ — أَصْدِقَاءُ :

غَنِيٌّ — أَغْنِيَاءُ : نَبِيٌّ prophet أَنْبِيَاءُ .

فُعَلَاءُ is plural of فَعِيلٌ when it has become a noun:

أَمِيرٌ prince, commander أُمَرَاءُ : شَرِيكٌ partner شُرَكَاءُ .

أَفْعِلَةٌ is plural of nouns with three consonants and a long vowel in the second syllable : جَنَاحٌ wing أَجْنِحَةٌ :

طَعَامٌ food أَطْعِمَةٌ — رَغِيفٌ loaf of bread أَرْغِفَةٌ —

عَمُودٌ pillar أَعْمِدَةٌ .

مَفَاعِلُ is plural of مَفْعَلٌ or مَفْعَلَةٌ whatever the vowels may be :—

مَكْتَبٌ school, office, library مَكَاتِبُ — مَدْرَسَةٌ

school مَدَارِسُ — مَسْجِدٌ mosque مَسَاجِدُ — مِنْجَلٌ

sickle مَنَاجِلُ . أَقْرَبُ relative أَقَارِبُ .

مَفَاعِيلُ is plural of nouns with four consonants, two

syllables and a long vowel in the second whether they have the feminine ending or not. مِفْتَاحٌ key مَفَاتِيحُ — صُنْدُوقٌ box صَنَادِيقُ — مَمْلُوكٌ slave مَمَالِيكُ — تَصْوِيرٌ picture تَصَاوِيرُ.

فَوَاعِلُ is plural of فَاعِلَةٌ and sometimes of فَاعِلٌ

فَاكِهَةٌ fruit (considered as food) فَوَاكِهُ — صَاحِبَةٌ companion صَوَاحِبُ — فَارِسٌ rider فَوَارِسُ.

فَعَائِلُ is plural of feminine nouns with three consonants and a long vowel in the second syllable.

فَضِيلَةٌ virtue فَضَائِلُ — رِسَالَةٌ letter رَسَائِلُ — رَذِيلَةٌ vice رَذَائِلُ.

فِعَلٌ is plural of فِعْلَةٌ.

قِطْعَةٌ piece قِطَعٌ — سِيرَةٌ manner of walking, character سِيَرٌ.

فُعَلٌ is plural of فُعْلَةٌ.

رُكْبَةٌ knee رُكَبٌ — تُحْفَةٌ gift تُحَفٌ.

All broken plurals are grammatically collective nouns in the feminine singular; consequently they may be construed with feminine singular adjectives.

نِسَاءٌ حَسَنَةٌ or نِسَاءٌ حَسَنَاتٌ fair women

رِجَالٌ كَبِيرَةٌ — كَبِيرُونَ — كِبَارٌ important men

(كبار is a broken plural of كبير generally used of persons.)

Second declension.—Several of the broken plurals end in *u* without nunation. These and similar nouns form the second declension which has two case endings, *u* for the nominative and *a* for the oblique, when they are indefinite. When definite, they have the three terminations of the first declension.

Nominative.	Accusative.	Genitive.
مَدَارِسُ	مَدَارِسَ .	
اَلْمَدَارِسُ	اَلْمَدَارِسَ	اَلْمَدَارِسِ

(The second declension has *a* in the oblique case while the sound feminine plural has *i*.)

All proper nouns, which end in ة, belong to the second declension.

Nouns which end in *a:*, whether written with *alif* or *y*, are indeclinable.

شَكْوَى complaint; دُنْيَا world.

The *a:* in these words is a feminine ending which is spelt with *y*, unless the third radical is *y* when *alif* is used for variety. The same ending occurs in the 'elative adjective'.

Number

There are three numbers, singular, dual, and plural.

The dual is formed by cutting off the case ending from the singular and adding اَنِ *a:ni* for the nominative and ـَيْنِ *ayni* for the accusative or genitive. There is no nunation. When a noun has only one form for these two cases, it is convenient to call it the oblique case.

عَيْنٌ *ʕaynun* eye, spring (of water); عَيْنَانِ *ʕayna:ni*; عَيْنَيْنِ *ʕaynayni*.

قِطْعَةٌ *qiṭʕatun* piece; قِطْعَتَانِ *qiṭʕata:ni*; قِطْعَتَيْنِ *qiṭʕatayni*.

The construct state is made by cutting off the *ni* :—

عَيْنَا ٱلْبِنْتِ *ʕaynalbinti* the (two) eyes of the girl. The *a:* is shortened in liaison.

عَيْنَيِ ٱلْبِنْتِ *ʕaynayilbinti*. The diphthong resolved in liaison.

Plural.—There are two ways of forming the plural, the sound or external and the broken or internal.

The external plural of nouns with the feminine ending is made by lengthening the *a* before the *t* which is then written as *t*, not as *h* with dots.

خَادِمَةٌ *xa:dimatun* maid servant; خَادِمَاتٌ *xa:dima:tun*, maids. This plural has two cases, *u* for the nominative, *i* for the oblique. It takes nunation.

Masculine plural.—Most participles and a few nouns make an external plural by cutting off the case ending and adding *u:na* for the nominative and *i:na* for the oblique case. There is no nunation. Note the alternation of vowels in the dual and the masculine plural.

خَادِمٌ *xa:dimun* servant; خَادِمُونَ *xa:dimu:na*;

خَادِمِينَ *xa:dimi:na.*

The construct state is formed by cutting off *na.*

خَادِمِي الطبيب خَادِمُو الطَّبِيبِ *xa:dimuttvbi:bi* *xa:dimittvbi:bi* the servants of the doctor. The long vowels are shortened in liaison. Adjectives agreeing with the external masculine plural usually take the external plural themselves.

Broken plural.—Nearly all masculine and many feminine nouns use the broken plural. This is made by a change in the word. No rules can be given for the simplest nouns and the plural must be learnt with the singular, it is all memory work. Many nouns have more than one plural; as a rule one form is the favourite or one form may be allotted to a special meaning.

عَبْدٌ *ʕabdun* slave, servant; عَبِيدٌ *ʕabi:dun* slaves;

عِبَادٌ *ʕiba:dun* slaves of God, worshippers, men.

All. There is no adjective meaning *all* which has to be expressed by كُلٌّ *kullun,* totality. Of course, this governs the genitive.

كُلُّ رَجُلٍ *kullu rajulin* every man;

كُلُّ الرِّجَالِ *kullurrija:li* all the men.

As the accusative is the adverbial case so :—

كُلَّ يَوْمٍ *kulla yawmin,* every day, daily;

كُلَّ الْيَوْمِ *kullalyaumi* all day long.

وَ *wa* 'and' is written with the following word. It was enough for the Arabs to join two contrasting phrases by 'and' where we must use 'but'.

Gender

There are two genders, masculine and feminine, so gender is not co-extensive with sex as it is in English.

The commonest feminine ending is *at*, with case ending and nunation, which is written with the dotted *h* ـَةٌ.

Some nouns and all the adjectives, which have so far been mentioned, form a feminine in this way; though most feminine nouns have no masculine correlative.

كَبِيرَةٌ *kabi:ratun* big; مَلِكَةٌ *malikatun* queen;

جَارِيَةٌ *ja:riyatun* girl; قِطْعَةٌ *qitʕatun* piece.

Two nouns have *t* as feminine ending :—

بِنْتٌ *bintun* daughter, girl; أُخْتٌ *ʔuxtun* sister.

Names of males are masculine even when they have the feminine ending. Otherwise all nouns with the feminine ending are feminine. Names of females, those of towns and countries and some collectives are feminine.

Some feminine nouns have no feminine ending: names of females :—

أُمٌّ *ʔummun* mother; عَرُوسٌ *ʕaru:sun* bride;

عَجُوزٌ *ʕaju:zun* old woman; أَتَانٌ *ʔata:nun* she ass.

Names of towns and countries :—

مِصْرُ *misru*, Egypt, Cairo (no nunation) ;

اَلشَّامُ *aʃʃa:mu*, Syria, Damascus.

Parts of the body which occur in pairs :—

يَدٌ *yadun* hand ; عَيْنٌ *ʕaynun* eye ;

قَدَمٌ *qadamun* foot, leg ; رِجْلٌ *rijlun* foot, leg ;

سَاقٌ *sa:qun* leg.

Some everyday words though no reason can be given :—

أَرْضٌ *ʔarđun* earth ; شَمْسٌ *ʃamsun* sun ;

خَمْرٌ *xamrun* wine ; نَارٌ *na:run* fire ;

دَارٌ *da:run* house ; نَفْسٌ *nafsun* soul ;

رِيحٌ *ri:ħun* wind ; سُوقٌ *su:qun* street of shops, bazaar.

The feminine ending has other uses. From collective nouns it forms a noun of unity, a singular :—

شَجَرٌ *ʃajarun* trees ; شَجَرَةٌ *ʃajáratun* a tree.

It forms emphatic nouns :—

عَلَّامٌ *ʕalla:mun* a learned man ; عَلَّامَةٌ *ʕalla:matun* very learned ; perhaps under this head comes خَلِيفَةٌ *xali:fatun* deputy, caliph.

Vocative.—If the noun has the article, it is put in the nominative and أَيُّهَا *ʔayyuha:* is prefixed; أَيُّهَا ٱلْمَلِكُ *ʔayyuhalmaliku* O king; before a feminine noun أَيَّتُهَا *ʔayyatuha:* is used. If the noun stands alone, it is put in the nominative without nunation and the exclamatory particle is يَا *ya:*.

يَا وَلَدُ *ya: waladu* O boy; يَا جَارِيَةُ *ya: ja:riyatu* O girl. Proper names, which have the definitive article, lose it after *ya:*; يَا شَامُ *ya: ʃa:mu* O Syria.

Cases

There are three cases; the familiar names, nominative, accusative, and genitive fit them well though the use of the accusative and genitive is wider than in English. Nouns of both genders which have nunation, have three case endings: *u* nominative, *a* accusative, and *i* genitive. Indefinite masculine nouns add *alif* to the accusative unless the word ends in *ʔ* preceded by *a:*. This *alif* is a letter of prolongation and is due to the fact that in Mecca a final *an* was often pronounced *a:*.

	Nominative.	Accusative.	Genitive.
moon	قَمَرٌ	قَمَرًا	قَمَرٍ
	qvmarun	*qvmaran*	*qvmarin*
	اَلْقَمَرُ	اَلْقَمَرَ	اَلْقَمَرِ
	alqvmaru	*alqvmara*	*alqvmari*

clothing	كِسَاءٌ	كِسَاءً	كِسَاءٍ
	kisa:ʔun	*kisa:ʔan*	*kisa:ʔin*
garden (now paradise)	جَنَّةٌ	جَنَّةً	جَنَّةٍ
	jannatun	*jannatan*	*jannatin*
	اَلْجَنَّةُ	اَلْجَنَّةَ	اَلْجَنَّةِ
	aljannatu	*aljannata*	*aljannati*

Construct state.—When one noun governs another in the genitive, the first is said to be in the construct state. The governing noun comes first and loses nunation:

بَيْتُ رَجُلٍ *baytu rajulin* a house of a man;

بَيْتُ الرَّجُلِ *bayturrajuli* the house of the man.

The second noun being definitive makes the first definitive also. Most Europeans find it hard to accustom themselves to this. The first noun, being definitive by position, does not need and cannot have the definitive article.

Nothing can come between the construct and its genitive; hence the name. An adjective agreeing with the first noun must come after the second. If the construct is definite, the adjective must be definite also; there is only one way of making an adjective definite, giving it the definite article.

شَعْرُ اَلْبِنْتِ اَلْجَمِيلُ

ʃaʕrulbintiljami:lu the beautiful hair of the girl.

دار البنت الجميلة is ambiguous if the vowels are not added as the feminine adjective may refer to either noun.

A sentence like 'a house of the man' cannot be translated directly into Arabic, you must go a roundabout way:

بَيْتٌ لِلرَّجُلِ *baytun lirrajuli* a house (belonging) to the man.

Emphasis.—'The house is big' may be translated in two ways:—

اَلْبَيْتُ كَبِيرٌ *albaytu kabi:run.*

إِنَّ ٱلْبَيْتَ كَبِيرٌ *ʔinnalbayta kabi:run.*

To an Arab the second is slightly more emphatic than the first but it is a degree of emphasis which cannot be represented in English. *ʔinna* puts the subject into the accusative but it is best left untranslated. A degree of emphasis, which can be translated, is got by using *ʔinna* with the particle *la.* This *l* also appears in the definite article and in some demonstrative pronouns.

إِنَّ ٱلْبَيْتَ لَكَبِيرٌ

ʔinnalbayta lakabi:run the house is indeed big.

All prepositions, with one partial exception, govern the genitive. Those, which consist of one consonant, are written as one word with the word they govern.

بِ *bi* by, with ; لِ *li* to, for ; كَ *ka* as, like.

After *li* the *alif* of the definite article is omitted and, if the noun begins with *l*, the *l* of the article also.

بِٱلْيَدِ *bilyadi* by the hand ; بِٱللَّيْلِ *billayli* by (the) night ;

لِمَلِكٍ *limalikin* to a king ; لِلْمَلِكِ *lilmaliki* to the king ;

لِلَّبَنِ *lillabani* for the milk.

There is no verb 'have'; the idea is expressed by a preposition. 'The man has a book' can be said in three ways with shades of meaning :—

لِلرَّجُلِ كِتَابٌ *lirrajuli kita:bun* (the fact of possession).

عِنْدَ الرَّجُلِ كتاب	*ʕindarrajuli kita:bun*	he has it on him.
مَعَ الرَّجُلِ كتاب	*maʕarrajuli kita:bun*	

The subject can be indefinite because the predicate is a prepositional phrase.

God. إِلَاهٌ or إِلٰهٌ *ʔila:hun god* (pl. آلِهَةٌ *ʔa:lihatun*)

اَلْإِلَاهُ *alʔila:hu* is sometimes used for *God* but usually it is shortened to اَللّٰهُ *alla:hu.* Note the spellings بِاللّٰهِ *billa:hi* and لِلّٰهِ *lilla:hi.*

مِنْ *min* of, from becomes مِنَ *mina* before the definite article and مِنِ *mini* in any other liaison.

With مِنْ *min* and عَنْ *ʕan*, the *n* is assimilated to the *m* of a following monosyllable ; مِمَّنْ *mimman*, from whom ; مِمَّا *mimma:*, from what. After لِ *li*, ما *ma:* is often shortened ; لِمَ — لِمَا *lima* or *lima:*, for what, why.

Accusative.—This is the adverbial case, for true adverbs are few.

Cognate accusative.—The infinitive, usually qualified in some way, carries on the idea of the verb :—

ذَهَبَ ذَهَابًا سَرِيعًا

he went off a quick going (quickly).

أَخَذْنَاهُمْ أَخْذَ عَزِيزٍ

we laid hold on them the laying hold of a strong one = we took a good grip of them.

The infinitive may be left out :—

اُذْكُرُوا اللّٰهَ كَثِيرًا remember God much (often).

Extensions of this construction are :—

ضَرَبْتُهُ مَرَّتَيْنِ I hit him twice.

ضَرَبْتُهُ سَوْطًا I hit him with a whip.

Accusative of reason or cause.—It is the infinitive of a verb of sensation or thought referring to the same time as the main verb :—

لَا تَقْتُلُوا أَوْلَادَكُمْ خَشْيَةَ إِمْلَاقٍ

do not kill your children from fear of poverty.

Accusative of extent in time or place.—All nouns of time may be used in this way :—

ذَهَبَ لَيْلًا he went away by night.

سَكَنَ فِي مَكَّةَ سِنِينَ [أَيَّامًا]

he dwelt some years (days) in Mecca.

For place only names of direction, measure, and general words can be used :—

ذَهَبَ مِيلًا he went away a mile.

نظَرَ يَمِينًا وَيَسَارًا [شِمَالًا] he looked right and left.

جَلَسْتُ مَجْلِسَ زَيْدٍ ـ جَلَسْتُ مَكَانَ زَيْدٍ

I sat in Zaid's place.

but جَلَسْتُ فِي ٱلْمَسْجِدِ I sat in the mosque.

Accusative of nearer definition.—This is used with weights, measures, verbs of filling and such like ; it is always indefinite :—

هِيَ أَطْوَلُهُنَّ ذِرَاعًا she was the longest of them in arm.

رِطْلٌ عَسَلًا a *rotl* of honey.

مَلَأَ ٱلْكِيسَ ذَهَبًا he filled the purse with gold.

Accusative of accompanying circumstance.—It is indefinite and English would use the nominative :—

قَدِمَ ٱلرَّجُلُ رَاكِبًا the man advanced riding.

اُدْخُلُوا رَجُلًا رَجُلًا come in, one by one.

The accusative may refer to any part of the sentence :—

نظَرْتُ إِلَى زَيْدٍ جَالِسًا

I looked at Zaid as he was sitting.

دَخَلْتُ ٱلْبُسْتَانَ زَاهِرًا

I went into the garden when it was in bloom.

ضَرَبْتُ زَيْدًا رَاكِبَيْنِ

I hit Zaid when we were both mounted.

Genitive.—This is used more freely than in English; possession is only one of the ideas expressed by it. Examples will make the usage clear.

رِطْلُ عَسَلٍ a *roll* of honey.

كُرْسِيُّ خَشَبٍ a chair of wood.

سَمُّ سَاعَةٍ poison of a moment (instantaneous).

'My knowledge' means 'what I know'.

عِلْمِي means 'what I know' and 'what others know about me'.

In technical terms the English genitive is subjective, the Arabic may be subjective or objective.

فَخَرْتَ بِأَيَّامٍ لِغَيْرِكَ فَخْرُهَا

you boasted of days (battles) the boasting in which belonged to others.

We have just seen the genitive describing a noun; it can also describe an adjective:—

قَلِيلُ ٱلْعَقْلِ little of understanding, foolish.

In this construction the adjective, unlike the noun, can take the definite article:—

ٱلِابْنَةُ ٱلْحَسَنَةُ ٱلْوَجْهِ the girl, the pretty of face.
the girl with the pretty face.

Verbs

The verb has no tenses. Apart from the imperative, there are two finite forms which denote respectively completed and incompleted action. It is convenient to call them the perfect and imperfect, some prefer perfective and imperfective, remembering that these terms do not mean what they mean in English. Normally the perfect indicates a finished and therefore past act while the imperfect denotes an unfinished and therefore present or future act. The simplest part of the verb is the third masculine singular of the perfect which is used as the name of the verb; we speak of the verb 'to write', Arabs speak of *kataba* 'he wrote'.

The verb is highly developed but on lines foreign to us. By additions to the root modifications of the original meaning are expressed. The plain root is called the simple or first and the enlarged stems are also called by numbers.

It is convenient to call the vowel, which follows the second radical whether in the perfect or imperfect, the characteristic.

In this book a strong verb is one which comes from a root having three different radicals, neither of them being *ʔ*, *w*, or *y*.

Perfect of the Strong Verb, Stem I

Before reading the following notes, study carefully the perfect in Table I.

The perfect is made by the addition of suffixes to the root. Those of the second person are the same as the endings of the personal pronoun, and closely resemble the pronominal suffixes.

In the third feminine singular and dual the *t* is the feminine *t*.

a: is the sign of the dual as in the nominative of the noun.

u: is masculine plural as in the external nominative plural of the noun. The *alif* following this *u:* has no meaning but is always written after a plural *u:* in the finite verb; in some weak verbs it is useful for distinguishing the plural from the singular. It is dropped before a pronominal suffix.

In Stem I there are three classes of perfect فَعَلَ — فَعِلَ

— فَعُلَ ; the inflections are the same for all. فَعِلَ فَعُلَ are usually intransitive. Many verbs have more than one form.

هَلِكَ — هَلَكَ he perished.

With verbs denoting a state, the perfect must be translated by the English present. شَبِعَ 'he is satisfied (with food)', i.e. he has eaten enough and now does not want to eat more.

The third person singular of the verb may contain its own subject. شَبِعَ 'he is satisfied', شَبِعَتْ 'she is satisfied' are complete sentences. You can also say, شَبِعَ زَيْدٌ 'Zayd is satisfied'; شَبِعَتْ زَيْنَبُ 'Zaynab is satisfied'. All other parts of the perfect or imperfect contain their subjects.

One grammar gives twenty-one rules for the agreement of subject and verb. You can write correctly if you remember this much :—

If the verb comes before the subject, it is third masculine singular unless the subject is a woman or women and follows the verb immediately when it is third feminine singular.

If the subject comes first, the verb agrees with it.

Other agreements are possible but not necessary.

دَخَلَ ٱلرَّجُلُ ٱلدَّارَ وَخَرَجَ مِنْهَا

The man went into the house and came out of it.

دَخَلَ ٱلرِّجَالُ ٱلْبَيْتَ وَخَرَجُوا مِنْهُ

The men went into the house and came out of it.

لَبِسَتِ ٱلْعَجُوزُ ثِيَابَهَا وَخَرَجَتْ مِنْ حُجْرَتِهَا

The old woman put on her clothes and came out of her room.

لَعِبَتِ ٱلْبَنَاتُ ثُمَّ رَجَعْنَ إِلَى بُيُوتِهِنَّ [بُيُوتِهَا]

The girls played, then returned to their houses (homes).

both right	كَتَبَ إِلَى أُخْتِهَا زَيْنَبُ كَتَبَتْ إِلَى أُخْتِهَا زَيْنَبُ	Zaynab wrote to her sister.

Arabic does not distinguish between being and becoming ; thus لَبِسَ means both 'to wear clothes' and 'to put them on'.

The addition of pronominal suffixes makes no difference to the parts of the perfect except the second masculine plural and, sometimes, the second feminine singular.

The object suffix of the first person singular is *nī*.

كَتَبَهُ he wrote it ; بَعَثَتْنِي she sent me ;

دَخَلْتُمُوهُ you (pl.) entered it ; ضَرَبُوهُ they hit him ;

لَبِسْتِهِ you (fem. sing.) put it on, or لَبِسْتِيهِ.

A nominal sentence begins with a noun.

A verbal sentence begins with a verb.

This distinction is important because some particles must be followed by a noun and others by a verb.

The verb comes first unless there is a reason for some other order. The direct object of a transitive verb is in the accusative.

Most verbs, which are transitive in English, are so in Arabic ; many, which are intransitive in English, are transitive in Arabic.

The perfect has only one form which serves for indicative, conditional, and optative.

The imperfect has three besides the indicative (Table 1).

Subjunctive.—This is a suitable name for this mood usually follows a subordinating conjunction. The *u* of the indicative is changed to *a*; the *ni* and *na* of the two syllabled inflections are cut off; while the feminine plurals are not changed.

It is used after the conjunctions لِ and كَيْ ' in order that ' and also after أَنْ when that follows a verb expressing any sort of wish or purpose.

طَلَبَ مِنِّى أَنْ أَذْهَبَ إِلَى اَلْقُدْسِ

he sought from me that I should go to Jerusalem.

أَنْ with the subjunctive can always be replaced by an infinitive :—

طَلَبَ مِنِّى اَلذَّهَابَ الى القدس

Jussive.—This is formed by dropping the inflection *u* of the indicative; in other places it is the same as the subjunctive.

It gets its name because it provides the imperative for the first and third persons and the negative imperative for the second :—

اُكْتُبْ write; لَا تَكْتُبْ do not write;

لِيَكْتُبْ let him write; لَا يَكْتُبْ let him not write.

TABLE 1

STRONG VERB—STEM 1—ACTIVE

	Perfect	Imperfect Indicative	Imperfect Subjunctive	Imperfect Jussive	Imperfect Energetic	Imperative
sing.						
3 m.	كَتَبَ	يَكْتُبُ	يَكْتُبَ	يَكْتُبْ	يَكْتُبَنَّ	
f.	كَتَبَتْ	تَكْتُبُ	تَكْتُبَ	تَكْتُبْ	تَكْتُبَنَّ	
2 m.	كَتَبْتَ	تَكْتُبُ	تَكْتُبَ	تَكْتُبْ	تَكْتُبَنَّ	اُكْتُبْ
f.	كَتَبْتِ	تَكْتُبِينَ	تَكْتُبِي	تَكْتُبِي	تَكْتُبِنَّ	اُكْتُبِي
1 c.	كَتَبْتُ	أَكْتُبُ	أَكْتُبَ	أَكْتُبْ	أَكْتُبَنَّ	
dual						
3 m.	كَتَبَا	يَكْتُبَانِ	يَكْتُبَا	يَكْتُبَا	يَكْتُبَانِّ	

f.	كَتَبَتَا	تَكْتُبَانِ	تَكْتُبَا	تَكْتُبَا	تَكْتُبَانِّ	
2 c.	كَتَبْتُمَا	تَكْتُبَانِ	تَكْتُبَا	تَكْتُبَا	تَكْتُبَانِّ	اُكْتُبَا
pl.						
3 m.	كَتَبُوا	يَكْتُبُونَ	يَكْتُبُوا	يَكْتُبُوا	يَكْتُبُنَّ	
f.	كَتَبْنَ	يَكْتُبْنَ	يَكْتُبْنَ	يَكْتُبْنَ	يَكْتُبْنَانِّ	
2 m.	كَتَبْتُمْ	تَكْتُبُونَ	تَكْتُبُوا	تَكْتُبُوا	تَكْتُبُنَّ	اُكْتُبُوا
f.	كَتَبْتُنَّ	تَكْتُبْنَ	تَكْتُبْنَ	تَكْتُبْنَ	تَكْتُبْنَانِّ	اُكْتُبْنَ
1 c.	كَتَبْنَا	نَكْتُبُ	نَكْتُبَ	نَكْتُبْ	نَكْتُبَنَّ	

Active participle كَاتِبٌ.

As a positive imperative the jussive always takes the prefix لِ ; after وَ and فَ the لِ loses its vowel.

وَلْيَكْتُبْ and let him write.

The jussive has other uses which have nothing to do with the imperative.

Energetic.—Roughly speaking, it is formed by adding *anna* to the indicative ; but the individual forms must be learnt.

With the emphatic لَ it is used in solemn statements, especially after oaths. It is also used to express commands and wishes.

قَدْ حَلَفَ لَيَقْتُلَنَّ he had sworn, he will kill.

Note.—Arabic has no strict rules for indirect speech as have English and Latin.

Conditional sentences.—The conjunction is إِنْ 'if'; either the perfect or the jussive may be used in both parts of the sentence.

إِنْ فَعَلْتَ هٰذَا هَلَكْتَ
إِنْ تَفْعَلْ هذا تَهْلِكْ
} if you do this, you will perish.

إِنْ لَا 'if not' is often contracted to إِلَّا.

مَنْ and مَا, when indefinite pronouns, are often treated as conditional particles :—

مَن سَكَتَ سَلِمَ he who keeps silent is safe.

The imperative being a command, is an incomplete action and so connected with the imperfect. It has no prefixes and the inflections are cut short. The loss of the prefix makes a helping vowel necessary; this is *u* when the characteristic is *u* and otherwise *i*.

اُكْتُبْ write; اِسْمَعْ hear; اِضْرِبْ hit.

The imperative is confined to the second person and is affirmative only; a negative command is expressed differently.

It can take the object suffixes.

The active participle is كَاتِبٌ ; فَعَلَةٌ and فُعَّالٌ are common forms for the plural.

When derived from a transitive verb, it can take an object and, being a noun, it takes its object in the genitive case:—

طَالِبُو عِلْمٍ seekers after knowledge, scholars.

It is obvious that this participle easily passes into a noun or adjective.

The passive participle is مَكْتُوبٌ: the plural is مَفَاعِيلُ.

In themselves the participles contain no idea of time.

Infinitive.—There is no fixed form for the infinitive of the simple stem; فَعْلٌ is common but the infinitive of each verb has to be learnt.

Many verbs of motion have the form فُعُولٌ:—

خُرُوجٌ — دُخُولٌ — نُزُولٌ but ذَهَابٌ.

فَعِلَ usually has فَعَلٌ :—

فَرِحَ rejoice فَرَحٌ — غَضِبَ غَضَبٌ be angry

As the infinitive is a noun, it can govern a genitive which may be either subject or object of the verbal idea.

قَتْلُ زَيْدٍ the killing of Zaid.
the killing by Zaid.

When both subject and object are mentioned, the subject is put in the genitive and the object in the accusative.

ضَرْبُ خَالِدٍ ٱلْوَلِيدَ Khalid's hitting Waleed

بَعْثِى إِيَّاهُ my sending him.

The object can always be put in the accusative.

The object both of an infinitive or a participle is often introduced by لِ especially when the verbal noun is in the adverbial accusative.

قُمْتُ إِكْرَامًا لَهُ

I stood up to do him honour (Lesson 15).

The infinitive takes the place of the two English forms 'to write' and 'writing'.

It passes easily into an abstract noun and even into a concrete one.

وُجُودٌ existence (وَجَدَ 'find').

تَصْوِيرٌ picture (from a derived stem 'give shape to').

The derived are formed from the simple stem (consult Table 2) by additions of various sorts and express some modification of the original verbal idea. It is the custom in European grammars to number them, the simple stem being I. They have each only one variety, unlike I, and are made from فَعَلَ فَعِلَ and فَعُلَ.

The inflections are the same as for the simple stem.

The derived stems fall into four groups determined by the vowel sequence in the imperfect.

II is formed by doubling the second radical: كَتَّبَ impf. يُكَتِّبُ.

III by lengthening the first vowel: كَاتَبَ impf. يُكَاتِبُ.

IV by prefixing *ʔa* and dropping the vowel of the first radical: أَكْتَبَ impf. يُكْتِبُ.

The prefix of the imperfect has *u* and the characteristic is *i*. Note that in the imperfect of IV the *ʔ* is dropped though it reappears in the imperative, أَكْتِبْ.

V is made by prefixing *ta* to stem II: تَكَتَّبَ impf. يَتَكَتَّبُ.

VI by prefixing *ta* to III: تَكَاتَبَ impf. يَتَكَاتَبُ.

The imperfect has the vowel *a* throughout, except of course in the final inflection.

TABLE 2

STRONG VERB—DERIVED STEMS

Active	II	III	IV	V	VI
Perf.	كَتَّبَ	كَاتَبَ	أَكْتَبَ	تَكَتَّبَ	تَكَاتَبَ
Imperf.	يُكَتِّبُ	يُكَاتِبُ	يُكْتِبُ	يَتَكَتَّبُ	يَتَكَاتَبُ
Imp.	كَتِّبْ	كَاتِبْ	أَكْتِبْ	تَكَتَّبْ	تَكَاتَبْ
Part.	مُكَتِّبٌ	مُكَاتِبٌ	مُكْتِبٌ	مُتَكَتِّبٌ	مُتَكَاتِبٌ
Inf.	تَكْتِيبٌ	كِتَابٌ	إِكْتَابٌ	تَكَتُّبٌ	تَكَاتُبٌ
	تَكْتِبَةٌ	مُكَاتَبَةٌ			
Passive					
Perf.	كُتِّبَ	كُوتِبَ	أُكْتِبَ	تُكُتِّبَ	تُكُوتِبَ
Imperf.	يُكَتَّبُ	يُكَاتَبُ	يُكْتَبُ	يُتَكَتَّبُ	يُتَكَاتَبُ

Part.	مُكَتَّبٌ	مُكَاتَبٌ	مُكْتَبٌ	مُتَكَتَّبٌ	مُتَكَاتَبٌ
Active	**VII**	**VIII**	**IX**	**X**	**XI**
Perf.	اِنْكَتَبَ	اِكْتَتَبَ	اِحْمَرَّ	اِسْتَكْتَبَ	اِحْمَارَّ
Imperf.	يَنْكَتِبُ	يَكْتَتِبُ	يَحْمَرُّ	يَسْتَكْتِبُ	يَحْمَارُّ
Imp.	اِنْكَتِبْ	اِكْتَتِبْ	اِحْمَرِرْ	اِسْتَكْتِبْ	اِحْمَارِرْ
Part.	مُنْكَتِبٌ	مُكْتَتِبٌ	مُحْمَرٌّ	مُسْتَكْتِبٌ	مُحْمَارٌّ
Inf.	اِنْكِتَابٌ	اِكْتِتَابٌ	اِحْمِرَارٌ	اِسْتِكْتَابٌ	اِحْمِيرَارٌ
Passive					
Perf.	اُنْكُتِبَ	اُكْتُتِبَ		اُسْتُكْتِبَ	
Imperf.	يُنْكَتَبُ	يُكْتَتَبُ		يُسْتَكْتَبُ	
Part.	مُنْكَتَبٌ	مُكْتَتَبٌ		مُسْتَكْتَبٌ	

VII is made by prefixing *n* with liaison: اِنْكَتَبَ impf. يَنْكَتِبُ.

VIII by inserting *t* after the first radical; the form begins with liaison: اِكْتَتَبَ impf. يَكْتَتِبُ.

X by prefixing *sta* with liaison. This is really a form like VIII made from *saktaba* which does not occur in Arabic though it is found in other Semitic languages.

اِسْتَكْتَبَ impf. يَسْتَكْتِبُ

In this group the prefix of the imperfect has *a*, and the characteristic is *i*.

IX and XI cannot be made from anything, which we should call a verb; they denote colours, and are best treated with the doubled verb.

Summary.—The perfects have *a* throughout, except of course in liaison.

If the imperfect has five syllables, the fourth has *a*.

Few verbs have all the nine stems.

In good Arabic VII is not made from roots beginning with *ʔ*, *w*, *y*, *r*, *l*, and *n*.

In VIII partial or total assimilation occurs when the root begins with *t*, *θ*, *d*, *ð*, *z*, *ṣ*. *ḍ* *ṭ*, *ð̣*.

دَرَكَ	اِدَّرَكَ			overtake
ذخر	اِدَّخَرَ	or	اِذَّخَرَ	store up
زحم	اِزْدَحَمَ			crowd together
صنع	اِصْطَنَعَ			take into one's employment
ضرب	اِضْطَرَبَ			be confused

صنجع اِضْطَجَعَ or اِضَّجَعَ lie down

طلع اِطَّلَعَ know (survey from above)

ظلم اِظَّلَمَ or اِطَّلَمَ suffer wrong

Each stem has its own meaning or meanings.

II is

intensive : كَسَرَ break كَسَّرَ smash

causative (this is an encroachment on IV) :

عَلِمَ know عَلَّمَ teach

declarative : صَدَقَ speak truth صَدَّقَ say that one speaks truth, believe

denominative : كَبَّرَ say, 'God is very great' (اَللّٰهُ أَكْبَرُ)

III is

conative : قَتَلَ kill قَاتَلَ try to kill, fight

نَزَعَ take away نَازَعَ try to take away, quarrel

It takes as direct object the indirect object of I :—

كَتَبَ write كَاتَبَ correspond with

رَكِبَ ride رَاكَبَ ride with (a person)

It is always transitive.

IV is

causative : جَلَسَ sit down أَجْلَسَ set down

V is the reflexive of II and then passive:

فَرَّقَ divide (trans.) تَفَرَّقَ scatter (intrans.)

VI is

reciprocal: ضَرَبَ hit تَضَارَبَ hit one another, have a free fight

pretence: نَعَسَ sleep تَنَاعَسَ pretend to sleep

VII is reflexive, then passive: اِنْكَسَرَ be broken

هَزَمَ defeat اِنْهَزَمَ let oneself be defeated

VIII is
reflexive (sometimes passive):

جَمَعَ collect (trans.) اِجْتَمَعَ collect (intrans.)

X is to ask or think that the simple verbal idea should be done.

حَسُنَ be good اِسْتَحْسَنَ think good, approve

غَفَرَ pardon اِسْتَغْفَرَ ask pardon from (trans.)

It is almost causative:

خرج go out اِسْتَخْرَجَ extract from a mine, make productive, till.

It takes considerable ingenuity to fit many verbs into this scheme; thus كَلَّمَ speak to (trans.) تَكَلَّمَ speak (intrans.). Here are two sample roots:—

	خَلَفَ u. خَلْفٌ		سَلِمَ سَلَامٌ	
I.		remain behind		be safe, well
II.	خَلَّفَ	leave behind	سَلَّمَ	greet (denominative) make safe, protect, surrender (trans.)
III.	خَالَفَ	oppose	سَالَمَ	make peace with, treat peaceably
IV.	أَخْلَفَ	break (promise) (make your word lag behind)	أَسْلَمَ	submit turn Muslim
V.	تَخَلَّفَ	hold back from	تَسَلَّمَ	receive the surrender, turn Muslim
VI.	تَخَالَفَ	disagree with	تَسَالَمَ	make peace together
VIII.	اِخْتَلَفَ	differ, be different	اِسْتَلَمَ	kiss (the Black Stone)
X.	اِسْتَخْلَفَ	appoint a successor, take in exchange	اِسْتَسْلَمَ	submit keep to the middle of the road

فَ 'and' denotes a closer connection than وَ and may often be rendered 'so', 'then'. In a conditional sentence it cannot be translated. Sometimes it denotes a change of subject.

The inflection of the imperfect is by prefixes and sometimes also by suffixes. The first radical has no vowel.

The prefixes denote the person except in the third feminine singular and dual where the *t* is feminine. Elsewhere *ya* stands for the third person, *ta* for the second, *ʔa* for the first singular (cf. أَنَا) and *na* for the first plural (cf. نَحْنُ).

a: is again the sign of the dual; *u:* of the masculine plural (except in the first person); *-na* of the feminine plural (cf. أَنْتُنَّ هُنَّ and كَتَبْنَ).

The imperfect has three forms يَفْعَلُ — يَفْعِلُ — يَفْعُلُ but the inflections are the same for all of them.

فَعُلَ has the imperfect يَفْعُلُ (no exceptions) كَرُمَ يَكْرُمُ

فَعِلَ has the imperfect يَفْعَلُ (perhaps five exceptions) غَضِبَ يَغْضَبُ

فَعَلَ has any of the three forms but يَفْعَلُ usually occurs when one of the second or third radicals is a guttural consonant.

The word سَوْفَ or the particle سَ is prefixed to the imperfect when it is desired to show that it refers to the future.

It suffers no change when pronominal suffixes are added to it. It often denotes an act growing out of another.

'He came out and looked' may be translated خَرَجَ يَنْظُرُ

or خَرَجَ وَيَنْظُرُ.

The imperfect suggests a close connection of the two acts ;

خرج وَنَظَرَ suggests two unconnected acts, Thus the imperfect often refers to past acts, as in the preceding example, when the whole sentence refers to the past.

An imperfect linked to the main sentence by 'and' or a pronoun or bý both indicates an attendant circumstance :

دَخَلَ وَهُوَ يَضْحَكُ he came in and he was laughing.

he came in laughing—while laughing.

Interrogative Adverbs

أَيْنَ where, whither ? أَيْنَ أَنْتَ where are you ?

أَيْنَ تَذْهَبُونَ where are you going ?

مِنْ أَيْنَ whence ; مِنْ أَيْنَ خَرَجُوا (from) where did they get out ?

كَيْفَ how ? كَيْفَ حَالُكَ how is your condition ? how are you ?

كَيْفَ فَعَلَ رَبُّكَ how did your Lord act ?

These words make no change in the form of the sentence.

كَمْ how much ? how many ?

When it asks a question, it is followed by a noun in the accusative singular :—

كَمْ حُجْرَةً فِى الْبَيْتِ

how many rooms are in the house ?

كَمْ إِنْسَانًا فِي ٱلْجَمَاعَةِ

how many persons are in the company?

بِكَمْ دِينَارًا ٱلثَّوْبُ

for how many dinars is the costume?

When exclamatory, it is followed by the genitive of a singular or of a broken plural; if there is a verb, it is in the perfect.

كَمْ كَأْسٍ شَرِبْتُ—كَمْ كُؤُوسٍ

what a lot of cups I have drunk!

In both usages, كم may be followed by من with a genitive:—

كَمْ مِنْ حُجْرَةٍ فِي ٱلْبَيْتِ

how many rooms in the house?

PASSIVE

The passive (Tables 3, etc.) is made by a change of vowels inside the verb. The inflections are the same as for the active except the vowel of the prefix of the imperfect. In stem I the perfect is *kutiba* and the imperfect *yuktabu*. The same scheme holds good for the derived stems; if there are more than three syllables, the extra one has *u* in the perfect and *a* in the imperfect.

a: in the perfect of III and VI becomes *u:* in the passive.

The passive imperfect of IV is the same as that of I.

Hollow verb, stem I.—Some typical forms are put side by side to make the differences apparent.

w. active.	قَالَ	قُلْتُ	يَقُولُ	يَقُلْنَ	يَقُلْ
passive.	قِيلَ	قِلْتُ	يُقَالُ	يُقَلْنَ	يُقَلْ
y. active.	بَانَ	بِنْتُ	يَبِينُ	يَبِنَّ	يَبِنْ
passive.	بِينَ	بِنْتُ	يُبَانُ	يُبَنَّ	يُبَنْ

The passive can only be used when the agent is not mentioned.

'Zaid was killed' قُتِلَ زَيْدٌ

'Zaid was killed by Muhammad' cannot be translated into Arabic, which can only say: قَتَلَ مُحَمَّدٌ زَيْدًا 'Muhammad killed Zaid'.

If an active verb has two objects, the first becomes the subject of the passive and the second stays in the accusative.

وَعَدَنَا ٱللّٰهُ ٱلْحَيَاةَ ٱلْأَبَدِيَّةَ God promised us eternal life.

وُعِدْنَا ٱلْحَيَاةَ ٱلْأَبَدِيَّةَ we were promised eternal life.

A verb may take two pronominal suffixes provided that they do not both refer to the same person or thing. When both are third person they cannot be of the same number and gender; indeed, it is better to make one of them independent by using *ʾiyyaː*.

أَنْكَحَنِيهَا he gave her to me in marriage.

نُلْزِمُكُمُوهَا { (we make you stick to it). / we compel you to take it.

أَسْكَنَهُمُوهُ he made them dwell in it.

TABLE 3

STRONG VERB—STEM 1—PASSIVE

	Perfect	Imperfect Indicative	Imperfect Subjunctive	Imperfect Jussive
sing.				
3 m.	كُتِبَ	يُكْتَبُ	يُكْتَبَ	يُكْتَبْ
f.	كُتِبَتْ	تُكْتَبُ	تُكْتَبَ	تُكْتَبْ
2 m.	كُتِبْتَ	تُكْتَبُ	تُكْتَبَ	تُكْتَبْ
f.	كُتِبْتِ	تُكْتَبِينَ	تُكْتَبِي	تُكْتَبِي
1 c.	كُتِبْتُ	أُكْتَبُ	أُكْتَبَ	أُكْتَبْ
dual				
3 m.	كُتِبَا	يُكْتَبَانِ	يُكْتَبَا	يُكْتَبَا

f.	كُتِبَتَا	تُكْتَبَانِ	تُكْتَبَا	تُكْتَبَا
2 c.	كُتِبْتُمَا	تُكْتَبَانِ	تُكْتَبَا	تُكْتَبَا
pl.				
3 m.	كُتِبُوا	يُكْتَبُونَ	يُكْتَبُوا	يُكْتَبُوا
f.	كُتِبْنَ	يُكْتَبْنَ	يُكْتَبْنَ	يُكْتَبْنَ
2 m.	كُتِبْتُمْ	تُكْتَبُونَ	تُكْتَبُوا	تُكْتَبُوا
f.	كُتِبْتُنَّ	تُكْتَبْنَ	تُكْتَبْنَ	تُكْتَبْنَ
1 c.	كُتِبْنَا	نُكْتَبُ	نُكْتَبَ	نُكْتَبْ

Passive participle مَكْتُوبٌ.

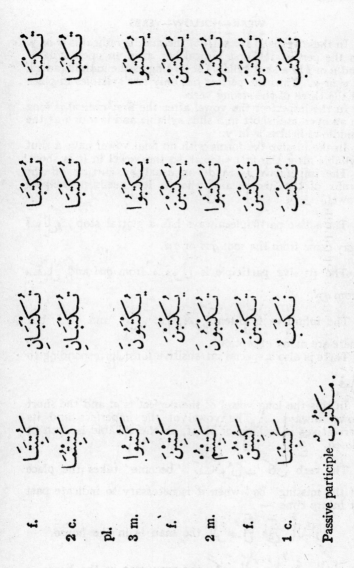

In these verbs (Tables 4—5) the middle radical is *w* or *y*. In the perfect the first radical has *a:* in an open syllable and *u* or *i* in a shut syllable according as the middle radical is *w* or *y*. Thus the perfect has only two syllables in place of the three of the strong verb.

In the imperfect the vowel after the first radical is long in an open and short in a shut syllable and is *u* or *i* as the middle radical is *w* or *y*.

In the jussive the forms with no final vowel have a shut syllable after the first radical, so the vowel in it is short.

The imperative is made as usual by cutting off the prefix of the jussive and what is left needs no helping vowel.

The active participle always has a glottal stop; قَائِلٌ may come from the root *qwl* or *qyl*.

The passive participle is مَقُولٌ from *qwl* and مَقِيلٌ from *qyl*.

The infinitive is often فَعْلٌ, i.e. قَوْلٌ and قَيْلٌ, but there are many exceptions.

There is also a special intransitive form corresponding to فَعِلَ.

In this the long vowel of the perfect is *a:* and the short vowel always *i*. The vowel of the imperfect and its derivatives is *a*, long or short, as the syllable is open or closed.

The verb كَانَ — يَكُونُ 'become' takes the place of the missing 'be' when it is necessary to indicate past or future time :—

اَلرَّجُلُ فِي اَلدَّارِ the man is in the house.

كَانَ اَلرَّجُلُ فى الدار the man was in the house.

يَـكُونُ اُلرَّجُلُ فى الدار the man will be in the house.

(A future particle is not needed, for the verb would not be used for the present.)

كان is also an auxiliary verb; the perfect of it is used with another perfect to express the pluperfect; قَدْ is sometimes added.

مَـاتَ اُلرَّشِيدُ بِطُوسَ وَكَانَ خَرَجَ إِلَى خُرَاسَـانَ

Rasheed died in Tus and (after) he had gone to Khurasan.

The perfect is also used with an imperfect to denote an act repeated in the past :—

كَانَ يَرْكَبُ فِي كُلِّ يَوْمٍ عِدَّةَ مِرَارٍ

he used to ride (rode) every day a number of times.

The imperfect with the perfect of another verb expresses the future perfect :—

يَـكُونُ زَيْدٌ كَتَبَ Zaid will have written.

When it is an independent verb, the subject is in the nominative and the complement in the accusative :—

يَـكُونُ اُلرَّسُولُ عَلَيْـكُمْ شَهِيدًا

the apostle will be a witness against you.

كُونُوا حِجَـارَةً أَوْ حَـدِيدًا be stone or iron.

Peculiar is the construction—

مَـا كَانَ لِ he is not the one to.

TABLE 4

HOLLOW VERB—MIDDLE W—STEM 1

	Perfect	Imperfect Indicative	Imperfect Subjunctive	Imperfect Jussive	Imperfect Energetic	Imperative
sing.						
3 m.	كَانَ	يَكُونُ	يَكُونَ	يَكُنْ	يَكُونَنَّ	
f.	كَانَتْ	تَكُونُ	تَكُونَ	تَكُنْ	تَكُونَنَّ	
2 m.	كُنْتَ	تَكُونُ	تَكُونَ	تَكُنْ	تَكُونَنَّ	كُنْ
f.	كُنْتِ	تَكُونِينَ	تَكُونِي	تَكُونِي	تَكُونِنَّ	كُونِي
1 c.	كُنْتُ	أَكُونُ	أَكُونَ	أَكُنْ	أَكُونَنَّ	
dual						
3 m.	كَانَا	يَكُونَانِ	يَكُونَا	يَكُونَا	يَكُونَانِّ	

f.	كَانَتَا	تَكُونَانِ	تَكُونَا	تَكُونَا	تَكُونَانِّ	
2 c.	كُنْتُمَا	تَكُونَانِ	تَكُونَا	تَكُونَا	تَكُونَانِّ	كُونَا
pl.						
3 m.	كَانُوا	يَكُونُونَ	يَكُونُوا	يَكُونُوا	يَكُونُنَّ	
f.	كُنَّ	يَكُنَّ	يَكُنَّ	يَكُنَّ	يَكُنَّانِّ	
2 m.	كُنْتُمْ	تَكُونُونَ	تَكُونُوا	تَكُونُوا	تَكُونُنَّ	كُونُوا
f.	كُنْتُنَّ	تَكُنَّ	تَكُنَّ	تَكُنَّ	تَكُنَّانِّ	كُنَّ
1 c.	كُنَّا	نَكُونُ	نَكُونَ	نَكُنْ	نَكُونَنَّ	

Active participle كَائِنٌ.

TABLE 5

HOLLOW VERB—MIDDLE Y—STEM I

	Perfect	Imperfect				Imperative
		Indicative	Subjunctive	Jussive	Energetic	
sing.						
3 m.	سَارَ	يَسِيرُ	يَسِيرَ	يَسِرْ	يَسِيرَنَّ	
f.	سَارَتْ	تَسِيرُ	تَسِيرَ	تَسِرْ	تَسِيرَنَّ	
2 m.	سِرْتَ	تَسِيرُ	تَسِيرَ	تَسِرْ	تَسِيرَنَّ	سِرْ
f.	سِرْتِ	تَسِيرِينَ	تَسِيرِى	تَسِيرِى	تَسِيرِنَّ	سِيرِى
1 c.	سِرْتُ	أَسِيرُ	أَسِيرَ	أَسِرْ	أَسِيرَنَّ	

Active participle سَائِرٌ.

MIDDLE W OR Y—INTRANSITIVE FORM

	Perfect	Imperfect				Imperative
		Indicative	Subjunctive	Jussive	Energetic	
sing.						
3 m.	نَامَ	يَنَامُ	يَنَامَ	يَنَمْ	يَنَامَنَّ	
f.	نَامَتْ	تَنَامُ	تَنَامَ	تَنَمْ	تَنَامَنَّ	
2 m.	نِمْتَ	تَنَامُ	تَنَامَ	تَنَمْ	تَنَامَنَّ	نَمْ
f.	نِمْتِ	تَنَامِينَ	تَنَامِي	تَنَامِي	تَنَامِنَّ	نَامِي
1 c.	نِمْتُ	أَنَامُ	أَنَامَ	أَنَمْ	أَنَامَنَّ	

Active participle نَائِمٌ.

صَارَ ـ يَصِيرُ 'become' and other verbs also take the complement in the accusative.

قَدْ with the perfect shows that it has the sense of the English perfect or pluperfect :—

إِنَّ ٱبْنَتَكَ قَدْ مَاتَتْ

your daughter has died (is dead).

قَدْ أَمَرَتْ بِٱلْبُخْلِ أُمُّ مُحَمَّدٍ

Umm Muhammad (name of a woman) had given an order about stinginess ; had told me to be stingy.

قَدْ with the imperfect means 'sometimes' :—

قَدْ يَعْلَقُ ٱلْقَلْبُ حُبًّا ثُمَّ يَتْرُكُهُ

the heart sometimes attaches itself to love, then leaves it.

The verb مَاتَ ـ يَمُوتُ 'die' is irregular ; in the perfect both مُتُّ and مِتُّ are possible.

Stems II, III, V, and VI are like the strong verbs ; 'w' verbs differ from 'y' roots :—

زَوَّجَ give in marriage ; تَزَوَّجَ marry ;

بَيَّنَ distinguish, make plain ; تَبَيَّنَ make plain to oneself, be plain ;

بَايَعَ do, receive homage ; جَاوَبَ answer.

In the other stems there is no distinction between the two classes. A long vowel appears in place of the middle radical just as in I; in the perfects that vowel is *a:* which is shortened where necessary to *a*.

In the imperfect of IV and X the vowel is *i:*, shortened where necessary to *i*.

In VII and VIII the imperfect unexpectedly has 'a' long or short as is required. إِنْقَادَ obey (let himself be led); إِخْتَارَ choose.

Indicative.	Jussive.	Imperative.	Infinitive.
يَنْقَادُ	يَنْقَدْ	اِنْقَدْ	اِنْقِيَادٌ
يَخْتَارُ	يَخْتَرْ	اِخْتَرْ	اِخْتِيَارٌ

Note the infinitive of IV and X; the middle radical is lost and the feminine ending 'at' is added as compensation.

إِقَامَةٌ IV اِسْتِقَامَةٌ X.

Some verbs have both strong and weak forms:—

أَرَاحَ — أَرْوَحَ give rest; اِسْتَرْوَحَ اِسْتَرَاحَ rest.

A few of the type فَعِلَ have strong forms only:

سَوِدَ be black; أَسْوَدَ blacken;

but اِسْوَدَّ XI be black and سَوَّدَ II blacken are more common.

TABLE 6

HOLLOW VERBS W OR Y—DERIVED STEMS

Active	IV	VII	VIII	X
Perf.				
3 s. m.	أَقَامَ	اِنْقَادَ	اِخْتَارَ	اِسْتَقَامَ
2 s. m.	أَقَمْتَ	اِنْقَدْتَ	اِخْتَرْتَ	اِسْتَقَمْتَ
Imperf.	يُقِيمُ	يَنْقَادُ	يَخْتَارُ	يَسْتَقِيمُ
Imp.	أَقِمْ	اِنْقَدْ	اِخْتَرْ	اِسْتَقِمْ
Part.	مُقِيمٌ	مُنْقَادٌ	مُخْتَارٌ	مُسْتَقِيمٌ
Inf.	إِقَامَةٌ	اِنْقِيَادٌ	اِخْتِيَارٌ	اِسْتِقَامَةٌ
Passive				
Perf.	أُقِيمَ	اُنْقِيدَ	اُخْتِيرَ	اُسْتُقِيمَ

Imperf.	يُقَامُ	يُنْقَادُ	يُخْتَارُ	يُسْتَقَامُ
Part.	مُقَامٌ	مُنْقَادٌ	مُخْتَارٌ	مُسْتَقَامٌ

STEM 1—PASSIVE

	Perfect	Imperfect Indicative	Imperfect Subjunctive	Jussive
sing.				
3 m.	قِيلَ	يُقَالُ	يُقَالَ	يُقَلْ
2 f.	قِلْتِ	تُقَالِينَ	تُقَالِى	تُقَالِى
pl.				
3 f.	قِلْنَ	يُقَلْنَ	يُقَلْنَ	يُقَلْنَ
2 m.	قِلْتُمْ	تُقَالُونَ	تُقَالُوا	تُقَالُوا

These verbs are regular according to both the classes to which they belong, except for occasional aberrations. The pronunciation is easy though the writing may cause difficulty. Here follow a few typical verbs.

Hollow and Hamza

Root اول 'return'

أُلْ يَؤُلْ يَؤُولُ أُلْتَ آلَ

Root جيء 'come'

جِئْ يَجِئْ يَجِيءُ جِئْتَ جَاءَ

The active participle is جَاءٍ اَلْجَائِي

Hamza and third 'y'

أَتَى 'come': the perfect is regular.

Imperfect يَأْتِي jussive يَأْتِ imperative اِيتِ and فَأْتِ.

رَأَى 'see': the perfect is regular.

In the imperfect the hamza is dropped :—

يَرَيْنَ يَرَوْنَ يَرَيَانِ تَرَيْنَ يَرَى

As in رَضِيَ the second feminine singular has the same form as the second feminine plural.

In IV the hamza is also dropped :—

perfect أَرَيْتَ أَرَتْ أَرَى

imperfect يُرُونَ تُرِينَ يُرِى

jussive يُرِ imperative أَرِ

The active participle I رَاءٍ and IV مُرٍ

Infinitive I رُؤْيَةٌ or رَأْىٌ ; IV إِرَاءَةٌ .

In verbs third weak with 'w' or 'y' as second radical the second is usually treated as a strong consonant.

حَيِىَ 'live' is irregular in places.

I may be treated as a doubled verb حَىَّ .

II. The infinitive is like that of a doubled verb with the feminine ending as compensation تَحِيَّةٌ .

X, when it means 'be ashamed', may be shortened :—

perfect اِسْتَحْيَيْتَ ـ اِسْتَحَى

imperfect يَسْتَحْوُنَ ـ يَسْتَحِى

First 'w' and third 'y'

وَفَى 'accomplish, fulfil'; the perfect is regular :—

imperfect يَفِينَ يَفُونَ يَفِيَانِ تَفِينَ يَفِى

imperative فِينَ فُوا فِي فِ

active participle اَلْوَافِي ـ وَافٍ infinitive وَفَاءٌ

A weak form can only be identified by grammar and common sense.

يدعو must be singular and must come from دعا.

يدعوا is plural and may be يَدْعُوا from دعا or يَدَعُوا from ودع.

يجد may come from وجد and be any form of the imperfect; it may be يَجِدْ or يُجِدْ jussive I or IV from جَادَ يَجُودُ; and it may be يَجْدُ or يَجْدِ jussive of جدا or جدى.

فِيهِ may mean 'in it', 'of his mouth' or 'accomplish it', imperative singular feminine of وفى.

VERBS FIRST 'W' AND 'Y'

First 'w' (Table 7).
Deviations from the strong verb occur in the imperfect of I and in VIII.
If the characteristic vowel of the imperfect of I is or ought to be 'i', the 'w' is omitted.

وَلَدَ produce young; يَلِدُ imperfect; لِدْ imperative.

In some verbs a final guttural has turned this 'i' into 'a' but the 'w' is still omitted.

وَضَعَ	place	يَضَعُ	ضَعْ	وَضْعٌ
وَقَعَ	fall	يَقَعُ	قَعْ	وُقُوعٌ
وَدَعَ	leave	يَدَعُ	دَعْ	وَدْعٌ
وَزَعَ	restrain	يَزَعُ	زَعْ	وَزْعٌ

A few have 'i' in the perfect and in the imperfect contrary to rule.

وَرِثَ	inherit	يَرِثُ	وَفِقَ	find suitable	يَفِقُ
وَثِقَ	trust	يَثِقُ	وَرِمَ	be swollen	يَرِمُ
وَلِيَ	be near	يَلِي	(this is also third 'y')		

In the imperfect of IV the 'w' combines with the preceding 'u' to form a long vowel. From وَجَدَ find IV means 'cause to be findable' and then 'create': أَوْجَدَ — يُوجِدُ — أَوْجِدْ — إِيجَادٌ.

There is no VII.

In VIII the 'w' is assimilated to the 't':—

وهم اِتَّهَمَ suspect; وفق اِتَّفَقَ agree

TABLE 7

VERBS FIRST W AND Y

Active	IV		VIII		X	
Perf.	أَوْعَدَ	أَيْسَرَ	اِتَّعَدَ	اِتَّسَرَ	اِسْتَوْعَدَ	اِسْتَيْسَرَ
Imperf.	يُوعِدُ	يُوسِرُ	يَتَّعِدُ	يَتَّسِرُ	يَسْتَوْعِدُ	يَسْتَيْسِرُ
Imp.	أَوْعِدْ	أَيْسِرْ	اِتَّعِدْ	اِتَّسِرْ	اِسْتَوْعِدْ	اِسْتَيْسِرْ
Part.	مُوعِدٌ	مُوسِرٌ	مُتَّعِدٌ	مُتَّسِرٌ	مُسْتَوْعِدٌ	مُسْتَيْسِرٌ
Inf.	إِيعَادٌ	إِيسَارٌ	اِتِّعَادٌ	اِتِّسَارٌ	اِسْتِيعَادٌ	اِسْتِيسَارٌ
Passive						
Perf.	أُوعِدَ	أُوسِرَ	أُتُّعِدَ	أُتُّسِرَ	أُسْتُوعِدَ	أُسْتُوسِرَ

Imperf.	يُوعَدُ	يُوسَرُ	يُتَّعَدُ	يُتَّسَرُ	يُسْتَوْعَدُ	يُسْتَيْسَرُ
Part.	مُوعَدٌ	مُوسَرٌ	مُتَّعَدٌ	مُتَّسَرٌ	مُسْتَوْعَدٌ	مُسْتَيْسَرٌ

STEM I—PASSIVE

Perf.	وُعِدَ	يُسِرَ
Imperf.	يُوعَدُ	يُوسَرُ
Part.	مَوْعُودٌ	مَيْسُورٌ

Verbs of the forms فَعُلَ فَعِلَ are regular in the imperfect of I :—

وَجِلَ be afraid ; يَوْجَلُ impf. اِيجَلْ impv. but وَوْجَلْ

وَبُلَ be unhealthy يَوْبُلُ اُوبُلْ فَوْبُلْ

Some nouns from these roots lose the first radical :—

جِهَةٌ direction ثِقَةٌ reliability.

سَعَةٌ (width) wealth, ability.

Though only two radicals are visible, there is no doubt about the root. Feminine nouns from hollow roots have a long vowel in the middle : قَامَةٌ 'stature' ; those from a third weak root have a long vowel after the second radical : زَكَاةٌ 'act of sacrificing'. A few nouns from third weak roots are without the long vowel but they all have 'u' in the first syllable : لُغَةٌ 'language'.

Verbs first 'y'.

There are only a few of these and the variations from the strong verb are few.

Two verbs have two imperfects in I :—

يَبِسَ be dry يَيْبَسُ and يَيْبِسُ

يَئِسَ despair يَيْأَسُ يَيْئِسُ

Note the imperative I : يَسَرَ – يَيْسِرُ – اِيسِرْ be easy.

The imperfect and participle IV : يُوسِرُ مُوسِرٌ become rich.

In VIII assimilation occurs : اِتَّأَسَ despair.

DOUBLED VERBS

In these verbs (consult Tables 8 and 9) the second radical is the same as the third.

The variations from the strong verb can be summarized in three rules :—

1. When the third radical has a vowel, the second loses its vowel and the two consonants are written once with *shadda*.
2. When the third radical has no vowel, the second keeps its vowel and the two consonants are written separately.
3. In the imperfect, when Rule 1 applies, the vowel of the second radical is thrown back to the first.

Rule 2 applies, in the perfect, to the first and second persons and to the third feminine plural ; in the imperfect to the feminine plurals only.

(The word, contraction, is avoided for there is no reason to think that these verbs were originally strong.)

The jussive has two forms ; one is regular according to Rule 2, the other is short like the imperfect indicative. A final double consonant cannot be pronounced so a short vowel, usually ' a ', is added ; the result is that the jussive cannot be distinguished by form alone from the subjunctive. Both forms existed side by side.

The imperative may be formed from the short form of the jussive and then needs no liaison.

A long vowel between the second and third radicals prevents them from coalescing ; examples are the infinitives of stems II, VII, VIII, and X and the passive participle of I.

TABLE 8

DOUBLED VERBS—STEM 1—ACTIVE

	Perfect	Imperfect Indicative	Imperfect Subjunctive	Imperfect Jussive	Imperative	
sing.						
3 m.	رَدَّ	يَرُدُّ	يَرُدَّ	يَرْدُدْ		
f.	رَدَّتْ	تَرُدُّ	تَرُدَّ	تَرْدُدْ		
2 m.	رَدَدْتَ	تَرُدُّ	تَرُدَّ	تَرْدُدْ	رُدَّ	اُرْدُدْ
f.	رَدَدْتِ	تَرُدِّينَ	تَرُدِّي	تَرُدِّي	رُدِّي	اُرْدُدِي
1 c.	رَدَدْتُ	أَرُدُّ	أَرُدَّ	أَرْدُدْ		
dual						
3 m.	رَدَّا	يَرُدَّانِ	يَرُدَّا	يَرُدَّا		
f.	رَدَّتَا	تَرُدَّانِ	تَرُدَّا	تَرُدَّا		
2 c.	رَدَدْتُمَا	تَرُدَّانِ	تَرُدَّا	تَرُدَّا	رُدَّا	اُرْدُدَا

pl.						
3 m.	رَدُّوا	يَرُدُّونَ	يَرُدُّوا	يَرُدُّوا		
f.	رَدَدْنَ	يَرْدُدْنَ	يَرْدُدْنَ	يَرْدُدْنَ		
2 m.	رَدَدْتُمْ	تَرُدُّونَ	تَرُدُّوا	تَرُدُّوا	رُدُّوا	اُرْدُدُوا
f.	رَدَدْتُنَّ	تَرْدُدْنَ	تَرْدُدْنَ	تَرْدُدْنَ		اُرْدُدْنَ
1 c.	رَدَدْنَا	نَرُدُّ	نَرُدَّ	نَرْدُدْ	Active participle رَادٌّ.	

PASSIVE

sing.					
3 m.	رُدَّ	يُرَدُّ	يُرَدَّ	يُرْدَدْ	
2 f.	رُدِدْتِ	تُرَدِّينَ	تُرَدِّي	تُرَدِّي	
pl.					
3 f.	رُدِدْنَ	يُرْدَدْنَ	يُرْدَدْنَ	يُرْدَدْنَ	Passive participle مَرْدُودٌ.

TABLE 9

DOUBLED VERB—DERIVED STEMS

Active	III	IV	VI	VII	VIII	X
Perf.	رَادَدَ ـ رَادَّ	أَرَدَّ	تَرَادَدَ ـ تَرَادَّ	اِنْرَدَّ	اِرْتَدَّ	اِسْتَرَدَّ
Imperf.	يُرَادُّ	يُرِدُّ	يَتَرَادُّ	يَنْرَدُّ	يَرْتَدُّ	بَسْتَرِدُّ
Imp.	رَادِدْ	أَرِدَّ أَرْدِدْ	تَرَادَدْ	اِنْرَدِدْ	اِرْتَدِدْ	اِسْتَرْدِدْ
					اِرْتَدَّ	اِسْتَرِدَّ
Part	مُرَادٌّ	مُرِدٌّ	مُتَرَادٌّ	مُنْرَدٌّ	مُرْتَدٌّ	مُسْتَرِدٌّ
Inf.	رِدَادٌ	إِرْدَادٌ	تَرَادٌّ	اِنْرِدَادٌ	اِرْتِدَادٌ	اِسْتِرْدَادٌ
Passive						
Perf.	رُودِدَ	أُرِدَّ	تُرُودِدَ	اُنْرُدَّ	اُرْتُدَّ	اُسْتُرِدَّ
Imperf.	يُرَادُّ	يُرَدُّ	يُتَرَادُّ	يُنْرَدُّ	يُرْتَدُّ	يُسْتَرَدُّ

STRONG VERB—STEM IX

	Perfect S	Perfect D	Perfect P	Imperfect S	Imperfect D	Imperfect P
3 m.	اِحْمَرَّ	اِحْمَرَّا	اِحْمَرُّوا	يَحْمَرُّ	يَحْمَرَّانِ	يَحْمَرُّونَ
f.	اِحْمَرَّتْ	اِحْمَرَّتَا	اِحْمَرَرْنَ	تَحْمَرُّ	تَحْمَرَّانِ	يَحْمَرِرْنَ
2 m.	اِحْمَرَرْتَ	اِحْمَرَرْتُمَا	اِحْمَرَرْتُمْ	تَحْمَرُّ	تَحْمَرَّانِ	تَحْمَرُّونَ
f.	اِحْمَرَرْتِ		اِحْمَرَرْتُنَّ	تَحْمَرِّينَ		تَحْمَرِرْنَ
1 c.	اِحْمَرَرْتُ		اِحْمَرَرْنَا	أَحْمَرُّ		نَحْمَرُّ

Participle مُحْمَرٌّ. Infinitive اِحْمِرَارٌ.

Part.	مُرَادٌّ	مُرِدٌّ	مُتَرَادٌّ	مُنْرَدٌّ	مُرْتَدٌّ	مُسْتَرَدٌّ

Stems IX and XI of the strong verb are only special forms of doubled verb and present no difficulties (Table 9).

The derived stems follow the same rules; II is no exception, for the second radical is already doubled and no consonant can be tripled.

V is sometimes irregular, the third radical being changed into 'y' and resembling a verb third weak. تَظَنَّنْتَ becomes تَظَنَّيْتَ you think.

Peculiar is the change from قَصَصْتَ to قَصَّيْتَ you cut.

Other forms behave like hollow verbs: ظَلْتَ or ظِلْتَ from ظَلَّ remain أَحَسْتُ for أَحْسَسْتُ I feel.

Nouns from these roots also follow the same rules.

مَحَلّ (مَحَالّ) 'place' come from theoretical *maħlalun* and *maħa:lilu*; حَلَال (loosed) not taboo, lawful, permissible.

The connection of ideas is this:—

حَلَّ u. حَلّ loose, untie.

When the bedouin unties his baggage, he camps dwells so :—

حَلَّ u. حُلُول dwell.

The antithesis of loosing and binding is familiar from the Gospels :—

صَاحِبُ ٱلْحَلِّ وَٱلْعَقْدِ

the master of loosing and binding—holder of supreme power.

So حَلَّ i. حِلَّ be not taboo, be lawful, allowable.

The opposite of this is حَرَامٌ حَرُمَ be taboo, sacred,

unlawful. حَرَمَ i. or حَرِمَ a. حَرِيمٌ forbid, prevent.

The two senses appear in one sentence :—

سَفَكُوا دَمَ ٱلْحَرَامِ فِي شَهْرِ ٱلْحَرَامِ فِي بِلَادِ ٱلْحَرَامِ

they shed forbidden blood in the sacred month, in the holy place.

These verbs go back to a time before morality had been associated with religion.

In the last example a noun in the genitive case acts as an adjective :—

رِجَالُ ٱلسَّوْءِ evil men.

VERBS WITH THE GLOTTAL STOP

Verbs with the glottal stop (consult Tables 10–12) are regular in pronunciation, apart from a few freaks. There remains the difficulty of writing ; the rule of thumb given in the chapter on the alphabet and the following notes will help to remove this.

FIRST HAMZA

When two hamzas should occur in one syllable, the second drops and the vowel is lengthened. Thus *ʔaʔ* becomes *ʔa:*, *ʔuʔ* becomes *ʔu:*, and *ʔiʔ* becomes *ʔi:*. *ʔa:* is written with madda.

TABLE 10
VERBS FIRST HAMZA

Active	I	II	III	IV
Perf.	أَثَرَ أَسَرَ	أَثَّرَ	آثَرَ	آثَرَ
Imperf.	يَأْثُرُ يَأْسِرُ	يُؤَثِّرُ	يُؤَاثِرُ	يُؤْثِرُ
Imp.	أُوثُرْ إِيسِرْ	أَثِّرْ	آثِرْ	آثِرْ
Part.	آسِرٌ	مُؤَثِّرٌ	مُؤَاثِرٌ	مُؤْثِرٌ
Inf.		تَأْثِيرٌ	إِثَارٌ مُؤَاثَرَةٌ	إِيثَارٌ
Passive				
Perf.	أُسِرَ	أُثِّرَ	أُوثِرَ	أُوثِرَ
Imperf.	يُؤْسَرُ	يُؤَثَّرُ	يُؤَاثَرُ	يُؤْثَرُ
Part.	مَأْسُورٌ	مُؤَثَّرٌ	مُؤَاثَرٌ	مُؤْثَرٌ

Active	V	VI	VIII	X
Perf.	تَأَثَّرَ	تَآثَرَ	اِيتَثَرَ	اِسْتَأْثَرَ
Imperf.	يَتَأَثَّرُ	يَتَآثَرُ	يَأْتَثِرُ	يَسْتَأْثِرُ
Imp.	تَأَثَّرْ	تَآثَرْ	اِيتَثِرْ	اِسْتَأْثِرْ
Part.	مُتَأَثِّرٌ	مُتَآثِرٌ	مُؤْتَثِرٌ	مُسْتَأْثِرٌ
Inf.	تَأَثُّرٌ	تَآثُرٌ	اِيتِثَارٌ	اِسْتِئْثَارٌ
Passive				
Perf.	تُؤُثِّرَ	تُؤُثِرَ	اُوتُثِرَ	اُسْتُؤْثِرَ
Imperf.	يُتَأَثَّرُ	يُتَآثَرُ	يُؤْتَثَرُ	يُسْتَأْثَرُ
Part.	مُتَأَثَّرٌ	مُتَآثَرٌ	مُؤْتَثَرٌ	مُسْتَأْثَرٌ

TABLE 11

VERBS MIDDLE HAMZA

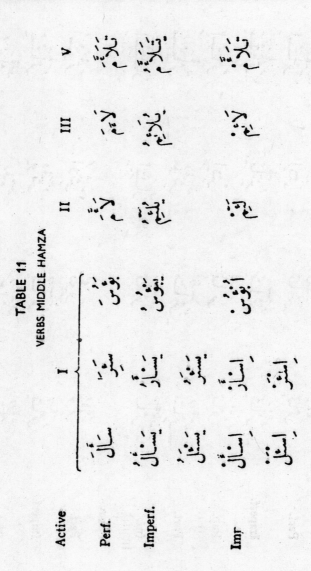

Active	I			II	III	V
Perf.	سَأَلَ	سَئِرَ	بَؤُسَ	لَأَّمَ	لَاءَمَ	تَلَأَّمَ
Imperf.	يَسْأَلُ	يَسْأَرُ	يَبْؤُسُ	يُلَئِّمُ	يُلَائِمُ	يَتَلَأَّمُ
	يَسَلُ	يَسَرُ				
Imr.	اِسْأَلْ	اِسْأَرْ	اُبْؤُسْ	لَئِّمْ	لَائِمْ	تَلَأَّمْ
	اِسَلْ	اِسَرْ				

Part.	سَائِلٌ	سَائِرٌ	بَائِسٌ	مُلْتَئِمٌ	مُلَائِمٌ	مُتَلَائِمٌ
Inf.	سُؤَالٌ	سُؤْرٌ	بَأْسٌ	تَلْئِيمٌ	مُلَاءَمَةٌ	تَلَاؤُمٌ
Passive						
Perf.	سُئِلَ			لُئِّمَ	لُوئِمَ	تُلُوئِمَ
Imperf	يُسْأَلُ			يُلَأَّمُ	يُلَاءَمُ	يُتَلَاءَمُ
Part	مَسْئُولٌ			مُلَأَّمٌ	مُلَاءَمٌ	مُتَلَاءَمٌ

TABLE 12

VERBS THIRD HAMZA

Active	I				II	III
Perf.	بَرَأَ	هَنَأَ	خَطِئَ	جَرُؤَ	بَرَّأَ	بَارَأَ
2 s. m.	بَرَأْتَ	هَنَأْتَ	خَطِئْتَ	جَرُؤْتَ	بَرَّأْتَ	بَارَأْتَ
Imperf.	يَبْرَأُ	يَهْنِئُ	يَخْطَأُ	يَجْرُؤُ	يُبَرِّئُ	يُبَارِئُ
Imp.	اِبْرَأْ	اِهْنِئْ	اِخْطَأْ	اُجْرُؤْ	بَرِّئْ	بَارِئْ
Part.	بَارِئٌ	هَانِئٌ	خَاطِئٌ	جَارِئٌ	مُبَرِّئٌ	مُبَارِئٌ

Inf.	بَرْءٌ	هَنْءٌ	خِطْءٌ	جُرْأَةٌ	تَبْرِئَةٌ	مُبَارَأَةٌ
Passive						
Perf.	بُرِئَ	هُنِئَ	خُطِئَ		بُرِّئَ	بُورِئَ
Imperf.	يُبْرَأُ	يُهْنَأُ	يُخْطَأُ		يُبَرَّأُ	يُبَارَأُ
Part.	مَبْرُوءٌ	مَهْنُوءٌ	مَخْطُوءٌ		مُبَرَّأٌ	مُبَارَأٌ

Active. Passive.

أَمَلَ hope يَأْمُلُ آمُلُ أُومِلَ

Imperative.

أُمُلْ hope أُومُلْ but فَأْمُلْ

أَسَرَ take captive يَأْسِرُ اِيسِرْ فَأْسِرْ

Two drop the hamza always in the imperative :—

أَخَذَ take يَأْخُذُ ـ خُذْ ; eat أَكَلَ ـ يَأْكُلُ ـ كُلْ

أَمَرَ drops hamza when the imperative stands alone but retains it after و and ف : مُرْ command but وَأْمُرْ .

Stem III

آكَلَ eat with يُؤَاكِلُ impf. آكِلْ impv. أُوكِلَ perf. pass.

Stem IV

آكَلَ feed. يُؤْكِلُ impf. أُوكِلُ 1 per. آكِلْ impv. إِيكَالٌ infin.

There is no VII.

Stem VIII

اِيتَزَرَ wear a loin cloth but فَأْتَزَرَ .

يَأْتَزِرُ impf. اِيتَزِرْ impv. but فَأْتَزِرْ .

Passive

أُوتُمِنَ was given authority; اَلَّذِى اُوْتُمِنَ he who was given authority.

أخذ assimilates ʔ to t: اتَّخَذَ.

MIDDLE HAMZA

The spelling is often not rigid: يَسْئَلُ — يَسْأَلُ.

The passive perfect I is سُئِلَ; this spelling seems to be derived from a dialect which used the form siːla.

سَأَلَ has also an irregular imperative سَلْ, jussive يَسَلْ.

The active participle I is like that of the hollow verb so

سَئِرَ	be left over	سَائِرٌ
يَسِيرُ — سَارَ	go	
يَسُورُ — سَارَ	jump	

THIRD HAMZA

Some of the spellings are not rigid :—

3 masc. dual perfect قَرَأَا — قَرَآ

2 fem. sing. impf. تَقْرَأِينَ — تَقْرَئِينَ

3 masc. plu. impf. يَقْرَأُونَ — يَقْرَؤُونَ

These verbs have 'w' or 'y' as third radical.

فَعَلَ. The third masculine singular of the perfect and the short forms of the imperfect have only two syllables instead of the three of the strong verb. In the simple stem of verbs third 'w' the third masculine singular of the perfect is written with *alif*, in those third 'y' and in all the derived stems of both classes it is written with 'y'. This probably points to an original difference in pronunciation but this has long been ignored. When the inflections of the perfect begin with a consonant, the forms are like those of the strong verb except that the weak radical forms a diphthong with the characteristic vowel. Elsewhere there is contraction for which no rules can be given. The third masculine dual cannot be contracted for the inflection is already long.

Most verbs with 'w' have 'u' in the imperfect and most with 'y' have 'i'. The radical combines with the characteristic to form a long vowel. When a back vowel is followed by a front vowel, the weak consonant reappears to separate them, as in the dual. When two back vowels come together, one is lost; the survivor is the vowel of the inflection for, if that were lost, the significant form would be destroyed. Thus تَدْعِينَ (root *dʕw*) second feminine singular; if the 'u' had survived, the resulting word would be تَدْعُونَ which is second masculine plural.

Again, يَرْمُونَ (root *rmy*) third masculine plural; if the 'i' had been kept, the result would be يَرْمِينَ which is third feminine plural.

The subjunctive explains itself.

The short forms of the jussive lose the letter of prolongation and with it all trace of the third radical.

The emphatic can only be learnt.
The imperative, of course, has liaison.

فَعِلَ. In verbs third 'w' there is partial assimilation of 'w' to 'y' so there is only one form for both classes.

Perfect. The characteristic 'i' is separated from 'a' of the inflection by the third radical and is lost before *u*:. When the inflection begins with a consonant, 'y' coalesces with the characteristic to form *i*:.

Imperfect. As in the transitive the short forms have only two syllables, the vowel of the second being *a*:. Before a back vowel, this is shortened and forms a diphthong. Before a consonant, it is resolved into the diphthong *ay*. Before *a*: (in the dual) it is resolved into 'a' and 'y' which begins the next syllable.

Passive. What has been said about the intransitive applies to the passive also.

Derived stems. Both classes become third 'y'.

Active participle. Contraction takes place in the nominative and genitive; the third radical and the case ending drop and nunation is given to the second radical :—

رَامٍ 'a shooter' (nom. and gen.) but رَامِيًا (acc.)

اَلرَّامِى 'the shooter' (nom. and gen.) but اَلرَّامِىَ (acc.)

This applies to all active participles of the derived stems and to all nouns from these roots with 'i' before the weak radical.

Something similar happens in some plurals :—

فَاعِلَةٌ has for plural فَوَاعِلُ.

So جَارِيَةٌ should have جَوَارِىُ but *iyu* is contracted to 'i' and nunation is added to indicate the contraction.

TABLE 13

VERBS THIRD W—CHARACTERISTIC A

	Perfect	Imperfect				Imperative
		Indicative	Subjunctive	Jussive	Energetic	
sing.						
3 m.	نَدَا	يَنْدُو	يَنْدُوَ	يَنْدُ	يَنْدُوَنَّ	
f.	نَدَتْ	تَنْدُو	تَنْدُوَ	تَنْدُ	تَنْدُوَنَّ	
2 m.	نَدَوْتَ	تَنْدُو	تَنْدُوَ	تَنْدُ	تَنْدُوَنَّ	اُنْدُ
f.	نَدَوْتِ	تَنْدِينَ	تَنْدِي	تَنْدِي	تَنْدِنَّ	اُنْدِي
1 c.	نَدَوْتُ	أَنْدُو	أَنْدُوَ	أَنْدُ	أَنْدُوَنَّ	
dual						
3 m.	نَدَوَا	يَنْدُوَانِ	يَنْدُوَا	يَنْدُوَا	يَنْدُوَانِّ	

f.	نَدَتَا	تَنْدُوَانِ	تَنْدُوَا	تَنْدُوَا	تَنْدُوَانِّ	
2 c.	نَدَوْتُمَا	تَنْدُوَانِ	تَنْدُوَا	تَنْدُوَا	تَنْدُوَانِّ	اُنْدُوَا
pl.						
3 m.	نَدَوْا	يَنْدُونَ	يَنْدُوا	يَنْدُوا	يَنْدُنَّ	
f.	نَدَوْنَ	يَنْدُونَ	يَنْدُونَ	يَنْدُونَ	يَنْدُونَانِّ	
2 m.	نَدَوْتُمْ	تَنْدُونَ	تَنْدُوا	تَنْدُوا	تَنْدُنَّ	اُنْدُوا
f.	نَدَوْتُنَّ	تَنْدُونَ	تَنْدُونَ	تَنْدُونَ	تَنْدُونَانِّ	اُنْدُونَ
1 c.	نَدَوْنَا	نَنْدُو	نَنْدُوَ	نَنْدُ	نَنْدُوَنَّ	

Active participle اَلنَّادِى ـ نَادٍ. Passive participle مَنْدُوٌّ.

TABLE 14

VERBS THIRD Y—CHARACTERISTIC A

	Perfect	Imperfect Indicative	Subjunctive	Jussive	Energetic	Imperative
sing.						
3 m.	رَمَى	يَرْمِي	يَرْمِيَ	يَرْمِ	يَرْمِيَنَّ	
f.	رَمَتْ	تَرْمِي	تَرْمِيَ	تَرْمِ	تَرْمِيَنَّ	
2 m.	رَمَيْتَ	تَرْمِي	تَرْمِيَ	تَرْمِ	تَرْمِيَنَّ	اِرْمِ
f.	رَمَيْتِ	تَرْمِينَ	تَرْمِي	تَرْمِي	تَرْمِنَّ	اِرْمِي
1 c.	رَمَيْتُ	أَرْمِي	أَرْمِيَ	أَرْمِ	أَرْمِيَنَّ	
dual						
3 m.	رَمَيَا	يَرْمِيَانِ	يَرْمِيَا	يَرْمِيَا	يَرْمِيَانِّ	

f.	رَمَتَا	تَرْمِيَانِ	تَرْمِيَا	تَرْمِيَا	تَرْمِيَانِّ	
2 c.	رَمَيْتُمَا	تَرْمِيَانِ	تَرْمِيَا	تَرْمِيَا	تَرْمِيَانِّ	اِرْمِيَا
pl.						
3 m.	رَمَوْا	يَرْمُونَ	يَرْمُوا	يَرْمُوا	يَرْمُنَّ	
f.	رَمَيْنَ	يَرْمِينَ	يَرْمِينَ	يَرْمِينَ	يَرْمِينَانِّ	
2 m.	رَمَيْتُمْ	تَرْمُونَ	تَرْمُوا	تَرْمُوا	تَرْمُنَّ	اِرْمُوا
f.	رَمَيْتُنَّ	تَرْمِينَ	تَرْمِينَ	تَرْمِينَ	تَرْمِينَانِّ	اِرْمِينَ
1 c.	رَمَيْنَا	نَرْمِي	نَرْمِيَ	نَرْمِ	نَرْمِيَنَّ	

Active participle اَلرَّامِي – رَامٍ . Passive participle مَرْمِيٌّ .

TABLE 15

VERBS THIRD W OR Y—CHARACTERISTIC I

	Perfect	Imperfect				Imperative
		Indicative	Subjunctive	Jussive	Energetic	
sing.						
3 m.	رَضِيَ	يَرْضَى	يَرْضَى	يَرْضَ	يَرْضَيَنَّ	
f.	رَضِيَتْ	تَرْضَى	تَرْضَى	تَرْضَ	تَرْضَيَنَّ	
2 m.	رَضِيتَ	تَرْضَى	تَرْضَى	تَرْضَ	تَرْضَيَنَّ	اِرْضَ
f.	رَضِيتِ	تَرْضَيْنَ	تَرْضَيْ	تَرْضَيْ	تَرْضَيِنَّ	اِرْضَيْ
1 c.	رَضِيتُ	أَرْضَى	أَرْضَى	أَرْضَ	أَرْضَيَنَّ	
dual						
3 m.	رَضِيَا	يَرْضَيَانِ	يَرْضَيَا	يَرْضَيَا	يَرْضَيَانِّ	

f.	رَضِيَتَا	تَرْضَيَانِ	تَرْضَيَا	تَرْضَيَا	تَرْضَيَانِّ	
2 c.	رَضِيتُمَا	تَرْضَيَانِ	تَرْضَيَا	تَرْضَيَا	تَرْضَيَانِّ	اِرْضَيَا
pl.						
3 m.	رَضُوا	يَرْضَوْنَ	يَرْضَوْا	يَرْضَوْا	يَرْضَوُنَّ	
f.	رَضِينَ	يَرْضَيْنَ	يَرْضَيْنَ	يَرْضَيْنَ	يَرْضَيْنَانِّ	
2 m.	رَضِيتُمْ	تَرْضَوْنَ	تَرْضَوْا	تَرْضَوْا	تَرْضَوُنَّ	اِرْضَوْا
f.	رَضِيتُنَّ	تَرْضَيْنَ	تَرْضَيْنَ	تَرْضَيْنَ	تَرْضَيْنَانِّ	اِرْضَيْنَ
1 c.	رَضِينَا	نَرْضَى	نَرْضَى	نَرْضَ	نَرْضَيَنَّ	

Active participle رَاضٍ ـ اَلرَّاضِي. Passive participle مَرْضِيٌّ.

The passive is inflected like verbs with characteristic 'i' in the perfect.

TABLE 16
VERBS THIRD W AND Y—DERIVED STEMS

Active	II	III	IV	V
Perf.	قَضَّى	قَاضَى	أَقْضَى	تَقَضَّى
Imperf.	يُقَضِّي	يُقَاضِي	يُقْضِي	يَتَقَضَّى
Imp.	قَضِّ	قَاضِ	أَقْضِ	تَقَضَّ
Part.	مُقَضٍّ	مُقَاضٍ	مُقْضٍ	مُتَقَضٍّ
Inf.	تَقْضِيَةٌ	مُقَاضَاةٌ	إِقْضَاءٌ	تَقَضٍّ
Passive				
Perf.	قُضِّيَ	قُوضِيَ	أُقْضِيَ	تُقُضِّيَ
Imperf.	يُقَضَّى	يُقَاضَى	يُقْضَى	يُتَقَضَّى
Part. m.	مُقَضًّى	مُقَاضًى	مُقْضًى	مُتَقَضًّى
f.	مُقَضَّاةٌ	مُقَاضَاةٌ	مُقْضَاةٌ	مُتَقَضَّاةٌ

Active	VI	VII	VIII	X
Perf.	تَقَاضَى	اِنْقَضَى	اِقْتَضَى	اِسْتَقْضَى
Imperf.	يَتَقَاضَى	يَنْقَضِى	يَقْتَضِى	يَسْتَقْضِى
Imp.	تَقَاضَ	اِنْقَضِ	اِقْتَضِ	اِسْتَقْضِ
Part.	مُتَقَاضٍ	مُنْقَضٍ	مُقْتَضٍ	مُسْتَقْضٍ
Inf.	تَقَاضٍ	اِنْقِضَاءٌ	اِقْتِضَاءٌ	اِسْتِقْضَاءٌ
Passive				
Perf.	تُقُوضِىَ	اُنْقُضِىَ	اُقْتُضِىَ	اُسْتُقْضِىَ
Imperf.	يُتَقَاضَى	يُنْقَضَى	يُقْتَضَى	يُسْتَقْضَى
Part. m.	مُتَقَاضًى	مُنْقَضًى	مُقْتَضًى	مُسْتَقْضًى
f.	مُتَقَاضَاةٌ	مُنْقَضَاةٌ	مُقْتَضَاةٌ	مُسْتَقْضَاةٌ

جَوَارٍ (nom. and gen.) جَوَارِيَ (acc.)

اَلْجَوَارِي (nom. and gen.) اَلْجَوَارِيَ (acc.)

Passive participle. In stem I verbs final 'w' have forms like مَدْعُوٌّ and final 'y' like مَرْمِيٌّ with assimilation because the resulting word cannot be confused with any other part of the verb.

When a noun from these roots has 'a' after the second radical, contraction occurs; the case ending is dropped and nunation put over the second radical. *Alif* is written in the 'w' roots and 'y' in those with 'y'.

فَتًى (فِتْيَانٌ) a man in the prime of life اَلْفَتَى

عَصًا (عِصِيٌّ) stick اَلْعَصَا

These nouns are indeclinable. All passive participles of the derived stems are of this form. مُلْقًى ـ مُصْطَفًى ـ مُسْتَلْقًى.

Infinitive. Stem II shortens the *i:* and adds *at* for compensation. تَسْلِيَةٌ.

Stem III. In the form مُفَاعَلَةٌ contraction occurs مُلَاقَاةٌ; the dotted 'h' shows that it cannot be a feminine plural.

Stems V and VI. The 'u' is assimilated to the 'y' and contraction occurs.

V تَلَقٍّ VI تَرَاضٍ

When the second radical has *a:*, the final radical becomes ʔ :—

رِدَاءٌ (أَرْدِيَةٌ) cloak (final ' y ').

كِسَاءٌ (أَكْسِيَةٌ) covering, dress (final ' w ').

Stems III, IV, VII, VIII, and X form their infinitives in this way.

اِسْتِلْقَاءٌ ـ اِبْتِلَاءٌ ـ إِلْقَاءٌ ـ لِقَاءٌ

أَفْعَلُ . The elative, like the imperfect, has only two syllables :—

أَعْلَى عُلْيَا عُلًى higher, etc.

In the feminine the radical ' w ' is usually changed to ' y ', so the *a:* is indicated by *alif* to avoid the repetition of ' y '.

Similarly أَعْمَى blind عَمْيَاءُ ـ عُمْيٌ .

فَعِيلٌ becomes غَنِيٌّ ـ قَوِيٌّ .

فُعُولٌ by assimilation becomes مُضِيٌّ infinitive of

يَمْضِي مَضَى .

Further assimilation occurs occasionally :—

عِصِيٌّ plural of عَصًا is the form فُعُولٌ as is قِسِيٌّ

the irregular plural of قَوْسٌ bow (weapon).

مَفْعَلٌ. Place nouns always have 'a' in the second syllable :—

مَنْجًى place of safety, refuge. Plural اَلْمَنَاجِي ـ مَنَاجٍ

Note.—The elative أَعْلَى has probably been influenced by the IV stem. The passive participles are inflected for number as follows :—

dual	مُصْطَفَيَانِ	مُصْطَفَيَيْنِ
plural	مُصْطَفَوْنَ	مُصْطَفَيْنَ

Negatives

There are several negatives, each with its special uses. The negative stands at the beginning of the sentence, except when it denies a single word.

إِنَّكَ عِنْدِي كَلَا شَيْءٍ

in my opinion you were as nothing.

لَا is 'no' and also 'not'.

A nominal sentence may be denied by مَا :—

مَا قَوْمٌ كَقَوْمِي

a tribe is not like my tribe—no tribe is like my tribe.

مَا هُوَ مِنَ ٱلْكِتَابِ

it is not from the Book (Koran).

A general negation may be expressed by لَا 'which denies the class'; the noun loses nunation and is in the accusative :—

لَا رَجُلَ فِي ٱلدَّارِ no man is in the house.

If there are two clauses, the nominative may be used in both :—

لَا خَوْفٌ عَلَيْهِمْ وَلَا فَزَعٌ

no fear is on them and no terror.

The defective verb لَيْسَ 'it is not' has no imperfect.

لَيْسَ — لَيْسَتْ — لَسْتَ — لَيْسَا — لَسْتُمَا — لَيْسُوا

— لَسْنَ, etc., is followed by a noun in the accusative or by

ب with the genitive :—

لَسْتُ بِعَالِمٍ — لَستُ عَالِمًا I am not learned.

Sometimes it is reduced in meaning to 'not' :—

لَسْتُ أَقْصِدُ ٱلْحَرْبَ I do not intend war.

Verbal sentences.—The past is denied by مَا with the perfect or by لَمْ with the jussive :—

لَمْ يَكْتُبْ — مَا كَتَبَ he did not write.

The future is denied by لَنْ with the subjunctive; here the subjunctive stands in a main sentence.

لَنْ يَكْتُبَ he will not write — he will never write.

ما with the imperfect denies the present :—

مَا يَكْتُبُ he is not writing (at the present moment).

لَا with the imperfect is a general negation and may refer to any time.

لَا يَكْتُبُ he does not write.

After another negative لَا may be used to continue a series of denials; the time is that of the first.

لَمْ يَدْخُلِ ٱلدَّارَ وَلَا نَظَرَ إِلَى شَيْءٍ فِيهَا
he did not enter the house and did not look at anything in it.

لَا with the perfect denies a wish :—

لَا رَحِمَهُ ٱللّٰهُ may God not have mercy on him.

لَا after an oath denies the future :—

وَٱللّٰهِ لَا فَتَحْتُ هٰذَا ٱلْبَابَ

by God I will not open this door.

لَا with the jussive is a negative command as was said in the previous lesson.

لَمَّا with the jussive means 'not yet' :—

لَمَّا يَكْتُبْ he has not yet written (but still has time).

بَلْ introduces a correction :—

اِضْرِبْ زَيْدًا بَلْ زَيْنَبَ beat Zaid ; no, Zainab.

لَا تَضْرِبْ زَيْدًا بَلْ زَيْنَبَ do not beat Zaid but (beat) Zainab.

غَيْرٌ is a noun meaning 'change'; in the construct state it means first 'other' and then 'not' :—

اَلْمُلُوكُ وَغَيْرُهُمْ the kings and others.

وَجْهُهُ إِلَى غَيْرِ مِصْرَ his face was not towards Egypt.

Adjective

Some of the common adjectival forms have already been mentioned.

فَعِيلٌ is often passive in meaning: قَتِيلٌ killed.

فَاعِلٌ the active participle is often used as an adjective or noun: عَادِلٌ just; شَاهِدٌ a witness, martyr.

مَفْعُولٌ the passive participle is used as an adjective: مَشْهُورٌ famous.

فَعُولٌ is intensive. جَاهِلٌ ignorant; جَهُولٌ very ignorant; كَاذِبٌ untruthful كَذُوبٌ a great liar; كَسُولٌ very lazy.

فَعْلَانُ (without nunation) the feminine is فَعْلَى: غَضْبَانُ — غَضْبَى angry; تَعْبَانُ — تَعْبَى tired; كَسْلَانُ — كَسْلَى lazy.

أَفْعَلُ has two meanings.

1. It denotes colours and bodily defects :—

	Masculine.	Feminine.	Plural
black	أَسْوَدُ	سَوْدَاءُ	سُودٌ
white	أَبْيَضُ	بَيْضَاءُ	بِيضٌ
red	أَحْمَرُ	حَمْرَاءُ	حُمْرٌ

The dual of the feminine changes the final *ʔ* into *w* ;

سَوْدَاوَانِ two black (women).

2. The elative, the 'adjective of superiority'. Arabic has only one form which does duty for both our comparative and superlative, it denotes intensity, the quality of the simple adjective raised to a higher power. The form is :—

Masculine.	Feminine.	Plural.
أَفْعَلُ	فُعْلَى	فُعَلٌ

Roughly, when this form is indefinite, it is comparative ; when it is definite, it is superlative.

When indefinite or when defined by a following genitive or pronominal suffix, the masculine is used for both genders and all numbers. When defined by the article, it is inflected for both gender and number. Of course, it is always inflected for case.

'Than' is expressed by مِنْ.

big كَبِيرٌ أَكْبَرُ كُبْرَى كُبَرٌ

اَلرَّجُلُ أَكْبَرُ مِنْ وَلَدِهِ

the man is bigger than his son.

دَارِى أَكْبَرُ مِنْ دَارِهِ

my house (fem.) is bigger than his.

شَوَارِعُ ٱلْعَاصِمَةِ أَنْظَفُ مِنْ شَوَارِعِ ٱلْقَرْيَةِ

the streets of the capital are cleaner than those of the village.

هُوَ ٱلْأَطْوَلُ فِى أَهْلِهِ

he is the tallest in his family.

هُوَ أَطْوَلُ ٱلْجَمَاعَةِ

he is the tallest of the party.

هِىَ أَطْوَلُهُنَّ ذِرَاعًا

she is the longest of them as to arm
= she has the longest arm of any.

هِىَ ٱلطُّولَى ذِرَاعًا

she is the longest in arm.

When the second and third radicals are the same, the forms of the elative are :—

few	قَلِيلٌ	أَقَلُّ	قُلَّى	قُلُلٌ
strong	شَدِيدٌ	أَشَدُّ	شُدَّى	شُدَدٌ

To make the elative from adjectives denoting colours or bodily defects, an adjective meaning 'strong' in the elative is used with the noun denoting the colour. The noun is in the accusative.

هٰذَا أَشَدُّ بَيَاضًا مِنْ ذٰلِكَ

this is more white than that.

There are two irregular elatives.

خَيْرٌ as a noun means any sort of 'goodness' and, as an adjective, 'better,' 'best.'

شَرٌّ as a noun means any sort of 'badness' and, as an adjective, 'worse,' 'worst.'

Feminines of the form فَعْلَاءُ belong, of course, to the second declension with only two case endings and those of the form فُعْلَى are indeclinable

Adverb

There are a few adverbs, mostly by-forms of prepositions; they are indeclinable.

بَعْدُ yet (in negative sentences); مِن بَعْدُ after, afterwards; مِنْ قَبْلُ ـ قَبْلُ before (time); مِنْ تَحْتُ ـ تَحْتُ below; مِنْ فَوْقُ ـ فَوْقُ above; حَيْثُ where; مِنْ حَيْثُ whence.

لَمْ يَمُتْ بَعْدُ he is not yet dead.

لِلّٰهِ ٱلْأَمْرُ مِنْ قَبْلُ وَمِنْ بَعْدُ

God's is the command, before and after = the business is in God's hands.

The infinitive takes the place of an adverb

Some English adverbs are replaced by verbs while the English verb takes a subordinate place as imperfect or participle.

Always.

زَالَ ـ يَزَالُ or بَرِحَ ـ يَبْرَحُ 'cease' with a negative:—

مَا زَالَ يَقُولُ ـ لَمْ يَزَلْ يَقُولُ

he did not cease talking = was always talking.

لَا يَزَالُ يَرْكَبُ he is always riding.

لَا تَزَلْ ذَاكِرَ ٱلْمَوْتِ always remember death.

Almost.

يَكَادُ ـ كَادَ be on the point of doing (never used alone).

كَادَ يَقْتُلُهُ he almost killed him; كِدْتُ أَفْهَمُ I almost understood.

Scarcely.

يكاد ـ كاد with a negative :—

لَا يَكَادُ يَتَحَرَّكُ he scarcely moves.

وَجَدَ قَوْمًا لَا يَكَادُونَ يَفْقَهُونَ قَوْلًا

he found a people who scarcely understood speech.

ذَبَحُوهَا وَمَا كَادُوا يَفْعَلُونَ

they sacrificed it but were nearly not doing so.

Again.

يَعُودُ ـ عَادَ 'return'; يَزِيدُ ـ زَادَ 'increase':—

عَادَ يَضْرِبُهُ he hit him again.

زَادَ يَشْتِمُهُ he abused him again.

At once, immediately.

لَبِثَ 'remain'; يَنْشَبُ ـ نَشِبَ 'stick to' with a negative :—

لَمْ يَلْبَثْ أَنْ قَالَ لَهَا at once he said to her.

لَمْ يَنْشَبُوا أَنْ بَلَغَهُمُ ٱلْخَبَرُ بِذٰلِكَ

they did not stick that: immediately the news about this came to them.

Soon, quickly.

أَوْشَكَ, IV of a verb first 'w', more usually the imperfect يُوشِكُ with أَنْ and the subjunctive; rarely the imperfect indicative. Three constructions are possible :—

يُوشِكُ أَنْ يَدْخُلَ زَيْدٌ ـ يُوشِكُ زَيْدٌ أَنْ يَدْخُلَ ـ

يُوشِكُ زَيْدٌ يَدْخُلُ

Zaid will soon come in.

The subordinate sentence ان يدخل زيد is the subject of the verb.

Perhaps.

The defective verb عَسَى of which only the perfect exists. Commonly the third masculine singular alone is used.

عَسَى أَنْ تَكْرَهُوا شَيْئًا

perhaps you do not like something.

Less common is the construction :—

عَسَى ٱلْأَيَّامُ أَنْ يُرْجِعْنَ قَوْمًا

perhaps the days will bring a tribe back.

There is also the particle لَعَلَّ which is construed like أَنَّ .

لَعَلَّ ٱللّٰهَ غَافِرٌ perhaps God is a pardoner.

لَعَلَّهُ يُسَافِرُ perhaps he will go on a journey.

In the morning.

أَصْبَحَ IV do, be in the morning, become morning.

أَصْبَحَ زَيْدٌ مَرِيضًا in the morning Zaid was ill.

أَصْبَحْتُ أَحْزَنُ عَلَى مُعَاكَسَةِ ٱلْأَيَّامِ بِى

in the morning I was grieved by the contrariness of the days (fate) to me.

The verb may be followed by a noun or by a sentence with the imperfect; often it loses all sense of time and means no more than كان or صار 'become'.

أَمْسَى (IV of a verb third weak) 'do, be in the evening' behaves just like اصبح .

In many other places the English adverb or adverbial expression becomes a verb in Arabic.

أَسْرَعَ ٱلذَّهَابَ

he made quick the going = he departed hurriedly.

أَبْعَدَ ٱلنَّظَرَ

he made distant the look = he looked into the distance.

A verbal sentence follows such phrases as :—

قَلِيلًا مَا ـ قَلَّ أَنْ ـ قَلَّ مَا seldom.

كَثِيرًا مَا ـ رُبَّمَا often.

طَالَ مَا it has lasted long.

قَلَّمَا رَأَيْتُ seldom have I seen.

قَلَّ مَا يَدُومُ وِصَالٌ seldom do (lovers') meetings last.

The numerals are the nightmare of a bankrupt financier.

1 أَحَدٌ fem. إِحْدَى is a pronoun.

وَاحِدٌ fem. وَاحِدَةٌ is an adjective.

Both these agree in gender with the noun to which they refer.

2 اِثْنَانِ construct اِثْنَا fem. اِثْنَتَانِ const. اِثْنَتَا

oblique اِثْنَيْنِ construct اِثْنَيْ fem. اِثْنَتَيْنِ const. اِثْنَتَيْ

This is a noun which agrees in gender with the noun numbered. Usually the dual takes its place but it is used n apposition for emphasis.

لَا تَتَّخِذُوا إِلَاهَيْنِ اثْنَيْنِ do not choose two gods.

3–10.	Used with the masculine:	with the feminine:
3	ثَلَاثَةٌ	ثَلَاثٌ
4	أَرْبَعَةٌ	أَرْبَعٌ
5	خَمْسَةٌ	خَمْسٌ
6	سِتَّةٌ	سِتٌّ
7	سَبْعَةٌ	سَبْعٌ

8	ثَمَانِيَةٌ	ثَمَانٍ acc. ثَمَانِيًا
9	تِسْعَةٌ	تِسْعٌ
10	عَشَرَةٌ	عَشْرٌ

These numerals are fully declined nouns, disagree in gender with the singular of the noun numbered, and put that noun in the genitive plural, if possible, a plural of paucity. (See below.)

ثَلَاثُ نِسَاءٍ three women; ثَلَاثَةُ رِجَالٍ three men.

When the thing numbered is definite, two constructions are possible :—

اَلرِّجَالُ الثَّلَاثَةُ or ثَلَاثَةُ الرِّجَالِ the three men.

Note.—The construct state of ثَمَانٍ is ثَمَانِي nom. and gen. ثَمَانِيَ acc.

Note.—ثَمَانِيهِنَّ the eight of them = the eight women.

11–12.	Masc.	Fem.
11	أَحَدَ عَشَرَ	إِحْدَى عَشْرَةَ
12	اِثْنَا عَشَرَ	اِثْنَتَا عَشْرَةَ (ثِنْتَا)
oblique	اِثْنَيْ عَشَرَ	اِثْنَتَيْ عَشْرَةَ

These numerals are not declined—except the part إِثْنَا and its variants. The noun is in the accusative singular. Both parts of the numeral agree in gender with the noun which is in the accusative singular.

Note the variations in the words for 'ten'.

13–19.

	With masculine:	With feminine:
13	ثَلَاثَةَ عَشَرَ	ثَلَاثَ عَشْرَةَ
14	أَرْبَعَةَ عَشَرَ	أَرْبَعَ عَشْرَةَ
15	خَمْسَةَ عَشَرَ	خَمْسَ عَشْرَةَ
16	سِتَّةَ عَشَرَ	سِتَّ عَشْرَةَ
17	سَبْعَةَ عَشَرَ	سَبْعَ عَشْرَةَ
18	ثَمَانِيَةَ عَشَرَ	ثَمَانِيَ عَشْرَةَ
19	تِسْعَةَ عَشَرَ	تِسْعَ عَشْرَةَ

These are indeclinable and govern the noun in the accusative singular. The unit disagrees in gender with its noun and with the ten.

20–30.

20	عِشْرُونَ	50	خَمْسُونَ	80	ثَمَانُونَ
30	ثَلَاثُونَ	60	سِتُّونَ	90	تِسْعُونَ
40	أَرْبَعُونَ	70	سَبْعُونَ		

These are ordinary external plurals and have the two cases; they take the thing numbered in the accusative singular.

In compound numbers between 21 and 99 the unit comes first.

100 مِـائَـةٌ (anomalous spelling) *miʔatun.* 200 is

مِـائَتَـانِ ; 300 ثَلَاثُ مِائَةٍ (sometimes written ثلاثمائة) with the hundred in the singular. مائة puts its noun in the genitive singular.

1000 أَلْفٌ . Note أَرْبَعَةُ آلَافٍ . The noun numbered is in the genitive singular.

Order of the numerals :—

ثَلَاثَةُ آلَافٍ وَثَمَانِى مِائَةٍ وَاثْنَانِ وَعِشْرُونَ 3822.

Ordinal Numbers.

	M.	F.		M.	F.
first	أَوَّلُ	أُولَى	sixth	سَادِسٌ	سَادِسَةٌ
second	ثَانٍ	ثَانِيَةٌ	seventh	سَابِعٌ	سَابِعَةٌ
third	ثَالِثٌ	ثَالِثَةٌ	eighth	ثَامِنٌ	ثَامِنَةٌ
fourth	رَابِعٌ	رَابِعَةٌ	ninth	تَاسِعٌ	تَاسِعَةٌ
fifth	خَامِسٌ	خَامِسَةٌ	tenth	عَاشِرٌ	عَاشِرَةٌ

These are ordinary adjectives and offer no peculiarities.

11–19. These are indeclinable.

	M.	F.
11th	حَادِيَ عَشَرَ	حَادِيَةَ عَشْرَةَ
12th	ثَانِيَ عَشَرَ	ثَانِيَةَ عَشْرَةَ
13th	ثَالِثَ عَشَرَ	ثَالِثَةَ عَشْرَةَ

etc.

For higher numbers the cardinal forms are used.

Note the compounds with 'first':—

nom.	حَادٍ وَعِشْرُونَ	اَلْحَادِي وَٱلْعِشْرُونَ
gen.	حَادٍ وَعِشْرِينَ	اَلْحَادِي وَٱلْعِشْرِينَ
acc.	حَادِيًا وَعِشْرِينَ	الحَادِيَ والعِشْرِينَ
	حَادِيَةٌ وَعِشْرُونَ	etc.

etc.

Four of the broken plural forms أَفْعَالٌ - أَفْعُلٌ - فِعْلَةٌ - أَفْعِلَةٌ are sometimes plurals of paucity, i.e. indicate a number less than ten. If a noun has two or more plurals and one of them is one of these four forms, it is used for numbers below ten.

بَقِيَ فِي ٱلسِّجْنِ شُهُورًا

he stayed in prison many months.

بَقِيَ فِي السِّجْنِ أَشْهُرًا

he stayed in prison a few months.

An undefined number between 3 and 10 is expressed by the noun بِضْعٌ (part): بِضْعُ رِجَالٍ a few men; بِضْعُ نِسَاءٍ a few women.

With larger numbers نَيِّفٌ is used: نَيِّفٌ وَعِشْرُونَ twenty odd.

Fractions.

$\frac{1}{2}$. نَصْفٌ.

$\frac{1}{3}$ to $\frac{1}{10}$ are expressed by فُعْلٌ (أَفْعَالٌ), e.g. ثُلْثٌ $\frac{1}{3}$.

Some fractions can be expressed by combinations of these words: ثُمْنُ رُبْعٍ $\frac{1}{32}$.

Others can only be expressed in words:—

سَهْمٌ مِنْ تِسْعَةٍ وَعِشْرِينَ سَهْمًا
قِطْعَةٌ مِنْ تِسْعٍ وَعِشْرِينَ قِطْعَةً } $\frac{1}{29}$

Distributives.

These may be expressed by repeating the numeral:—

فَرَضَ عَلَيْهِمْ أَلْفَيْنِ أَلْفَيْنِ he allotted them 2,000 apiece.

CARDINAL NUMBERS

One	ایک	Wâhed	واحد
Two	دو	Ithnan	إثنان
Three	تین	Thalathat	ثلاثة
Four	چار	Arbaat	اربعة
Five	پانچ	Khamsa	خمسة
Six	چھ	Sitta	ستة
Seven	سات	Sab'a	سبعة
Eight	آٹھ	Thamania	ثمانية
Nine	نو	Tiss'a	تسعة
Ten	دس	Ashra	عشرة
Eleven	گیارہ	Ihda ashar	احدى عشر
Twelve	بارہ	Ithna ashar	اثنا عشر
Thirteen	تیرہ	Thalathat ashar	ثلاثة عشر
Fourteen	چودہ	Arba'at ashar	اربعة عشر
Fifteen	پندرہ	Khamsat ashar	خمسة عشر
Sixteen	سولہ	Sittat ashar	ستة عشر
Seventeen	سترہ	Sab'at ashar	سبعة عشر
Eighteen	اٹھارہ	Thamaniat ashar	ثمانية عشر
Nineteen	انیس	Tiss'at ashar	تسعة عشر
Twenty	بیس	Ishroon	عشرون
Twenty one	اکیس	Wahed wa Ishroon	واحد وعشرون
etc.	وغیرہ	Ila akhirihi	الخ
Thirty	تیس	Thalathoon	ثلاثون
Forty	چالیس	Arba'oon	اربعون
Fifty	پچاس	Khamsoon	خمسون
Sixty.	ساٹھ	Sitoon	ستون
Seventy	ستر	Sab'oon	سبعون.

Eighty	اسی	Thamanoon	ثمانون
Ninety	نوے	Tissoon	تسعون
A hundred	سو	Myyah	مئة
A hundred and one	ایک سو ایک	*Myyah wa wahid*	مئة وواحد
A hundred and ten	ایک سو دس	*Myyah wa ashra*	مئة وعشرة
A hundred and eighteen	ایک سو اٹھارہ	*Myyah wa thamaniat ashar*	مئة وثمانية عشر
A hundred and Thirty	ایک سو تیس	*Myyah wa Thalathoon*	مئة وثلاثون
Etc.	وغیرہ	*Ila akhiriki*	الخ
A hundred	ایک سو	Myyah	مئة
Two hundred	دو سو	Mi'atàn	مئتان
Three hundred	تین سو	Thalath myyah	ثلاثمائة
Four hundred	چار سو	Arba myyah	اربعماية
Five hundred	پانچ سو	Khamsmyyah	خمسماية
Six hundred	چھ سو	Sitmyyah	ستماية
Seven hundred	سات سو	Sabeh myyah	سبعماية
Eight hundred	آٹھ سو	Thaman myyah	ثمنماية
Nine hundred	نو سو	Tissi myyah	تسعماية
One thousand	ایک ہزار	Alf	الف
Ten thousand	دس ہزار	Asharat alaf	عشرة آلاف
Twenty thousand	بیس ہزار	Ishroon alf	عشرون الف
One million	دس لاکھ	Maliyoon	مليون

ORDINAL NUMBERS

The first	پہلا	Al-awal	الاول
The second	دوسرا	Al-Thâni	الثاني
The third	تیسرا	Al-Thâlith	الثالث
The fourth	چوتھا	Al-Rabeh	الرابع
The fifth	پانچواں	Al-Khamés	الخامس
The sixth	چھٹا	Al-Sadés	السادس
The seventh	ساتواں	Al-Sabeh	السابع
The eighth	آٹھواں	Al-Thamen	الثامن
The ninth	نواں	Al-Taseh	التاسع
The tenth	دسواں	Al-Asher	العاشر
The eleventh	گیارھواں	Al Hadi Ashar	الحادي عشر
The twelfth	بارھواں	Al Thani Ashar	الثاني عشر
The thirteenth	تیرھواں	Al Thaleth Ashar	الثالث عشر
The fourteenth	چودھواں	Al Rabeh Ashar	الرابع عشر
The fifteenth	پندرھواں	Al Khames Ashar	الخامس عشر
The sixteenth	سولھواں	Al Sades ashar	السادس عشر
The seventeenth	سترھواں	Al Sabeh ashar	السابع عشر
The eighteenth	اٹھارواں	Al Thamen ashar	الثامن عشر
The nineteenth	انیسواں	Al Taseh ashar	التاسع عشر
The twentieth	بیسواں	Al Ishroon	العشرون
The twenty first	اکیسواں	Al Hadi wal ishroon	الحادي والعشرون
The twenty second	بائیسواں	Al Thani wal ishroon	الثاني والعشرون
The twenty third	تئیسواں	Al Thaleth wal ishroon	الثالث والعشرون
The twenty fourth	چوبیسواں	Al Rabeh wal ishroon	الرابع والعشرون

The twenty fifth	پچیسواں	Al Khames wal ishroon	الخامس والعشرون
The twenty sixth	چھبیسواں	Sades wal ishroon	السادس والعشرون
The twenty seventh	ستائیسواں	Al Sabeh wal ishroon	السابع والعشرون
The twenty eighth	اٹھائیسواں	Al Thamen wal ishroon	الثامن والعشرون
The twenty nineth	انتیسواں	Al taseh wal ishroon	التاسع والعشرون
The thirtieh	تیسواں	Al thalathoon	الثلاثون
The fourtieth	چالیسواں	**Al arbaoon**	الاربعون
The fiftieth	پچاسواں	**Al khamsoon**	الخمسون
The sixtieth	ساٹھواں	**Al sittoon**	الستون
The seventieth	سترواں	**Al saboon**	السبعون
The eightieth	اسی واں	**Al thamanoon**	الثمانون
The ninetieth	نوے واں	**Al tissoon**	التسعون
The hundredth	سو واں	**Al myya**	المائة
The thousandth	ہزارواں	**Al alf**	الالف
The milionth	دس لاکھ واں	**Al milyoon**	المليون

One half	آدھا	**Nisf**	نصف
One fourth	چوتھائی	**Roboh**	ربع
Three fourths	تین چوتھائی	**Thalathat arba'**	ثلاثة أرباع
One third	ایک تہائی	**Tholth**	ثلث
One fifth	پانچواں حصہ	**Khoms**	خُمس

One sixth	چھٹا حصہ	**Sods**	سُدُس
One seventh	ساتواں حصہ	**Sobo'**	سُبع
One eighth	آٹھواں حصہ	**Thomn**	ثُمن
One ninth	نواں حصہ	Toso'	تُسع
One tenth	دسواں حصہ	Oshor	عُشر
A couple	جوڑا	Zôj	زوج
A pair	جوڑا	Zôj	زوج
A dozen	درجن	**Dazzina**	دزينة
Half a dozen	آدھی درجن	**Nisf Dazzina**	نصف دزينة
A score	ایک کوڑی، بیس	Ishroon	عشرون
Double	دوہرا	Do'of	ضعف
Triple	تہرا	Thalathat adhaâf	ثلاثة أضعاف
Fourfold	چارگنا	Arba'at adh'âf	أربعة أضعاف
Fivefold	پانچ گنا	Khamsat adh'âf	خمسة أضعاف
Sixfold	چھ گنا	Sittat adh'âf	ستة أضعاف
Sevenfold	سات گنا	Sab'at adh'af	سبعة أضعاف
Eightfold	آٹھ گنا	Thamaniat adh'âf	ثمانية أضعاف
Ninefold	نو گنا	Tiss'at adh'âf	تسعة أضعاف
Tenfold	دس گنا	Asharat adh'âf	عشرة أضعاف
Hundredfold	سو گنا	Miat dho'f	مئة ضعف

DAYS OF THE WEEK

Week	أسبوع	alusboo'
Sunday	الأحد	alaḥaḍ
Monday	الإثنين	aliṭnayn
Tuesday	الثلاثاء	aṭṭalaaṭaa
Wednesday	الأربعاء	alarba'aa
Thursday	الخميس	alḳhamees
Friday	الجمعة	aljumaa
Saturday	السبت	alsabṭ
working day	يوم عمل	yoom amal
day off	يوم إجازة / يوم فرصة	yoom ijaazaa/ yoom fursaa
holidays/vacation	الإجازة	alajaaza
weekday	يوم في وسط الأسبوع	yoom fi wasṭil usboo
two days ago	منذ يومين	munḍ yoomayn
after three days	بعد ثلاثة أيام	baaḍ ṭallaṭ ayyaam
in two weeks time	بعد أسبوعين	baaḍ usbu'een

MONTHS OF THE YEAR

January	يناير/كانون ثاني	yanaayir/kaanoon ṭaanee
February	فبراير/شباط	fibraayir/shubaaṭ
March	مارس/آزار	maaris/aaḍaar
April	إبريل/نيسان	abreel/neesaan
May	مايو/ايار	maayoo/ayaar
June	يونيو/حزيران	yoonyoo/ ḥazeeraan
July	يوليو/تموز	yoolyoo/ṭamooz
August	أغسطس/آب	ugusṭus/aab
September	سبتمبر/ايلول	sibṭambir/aylool
October	اكتوبر/تشرين أول	ukṭoobar/ṭishreen awwal
November	نوفمبر/تشرين ثاني	noofimbir/ṭishreen ṭaanee
December	ديسمبر/ كانون أول	disimbir/ kanoon awwal
since last month	منذ الشهر الماضي	mund ashshahr almaaḍee.
during the next month	خلال الشهر القادم	khilaal ashshar alqaadim.
first July	أول يوليو	aww yoolyoo

PARTS OF DAY

morning/in the morning	**صُبح/في الصباح**	**subḥ!/fissabaaḥ.**
noon/at noon	**ظهر/لظهر**	**ẓuhr/liẓuhr.**
afternoon	**بعد الظهر**	**baaḍaẓẓuhr.**
day	**نهار**	**nahaar**
mid-day	**نصف النهار**	**nisfannahaar**
dawn/day-break	**شروق**	**shurooq**
sunset	**غروب**	**ghuroob**
evening/in the evening	**مساء/في المساء**	**masaa/filmasaa**
night/at night	**ليل/في اللّيل**	**layl /fil layl**
midnight	**نصف الليل**	**nisfal layl**
tonight	**الليلة**	**allaylaa**
today	اليوم	alyoom
yesterday	أمس	ams
tomorrow	بكرة/غدا	bukraa/ghaḍaa.

PROFESSIONS AND OCCUPATIONS

lawyer	محامي	muḥaamee
judge	قاضي	qaaḍee
jeweller	جوهري	jauharee
chemist	صيدلي	sayḍlee
vegetable vendor	خضري	khuḍree
fruit seller	فاكهي	faakihee
confectioner	حلواني	ḥulwaanee
banker	صيرفي	sayrafee
	أبو بنك	abu bank
blacksmith	حدّاد	haḍḍaaḍ
weaver	نسّاج	nassaaj
fisherman	سمّاك	sammaak
butcher	لحّام	laḥḥaam
cobbler	سقّاف	saqqaaf
cooli/porter	شيّال	shayyaal
engineer	مهندس	muhanḍis
writer	مؤلف	muallif
translator	مترجم	muṭarjim
interpreter	ترجمان	ṭarjumaan
journalist	صحفي	suḥufee
editor	رئيس تحرير	raees ṭaḥreer
cook	**طبّاخ**	**ṭabbaakh**

airhostess	مضيّفة	muḍayyifa
contractor	مقاول	muqaawil
worker	عامل	aamil
servant	خادم	ḳhaaḍim
driver	سائق	saaiq
goldsmith	صائغ	saaigh
poet	شاعر	shaair
teacher	مدرّس	muḍarri
professor	أستاذ	usṭaaḍ
clerk	كاتب	kaaṭib
accountant	محاسب	muḥaasib
book keeper	ماسك	maasik
watchman	مراقب	muraaqib
guard	حارس	ḥaaris
businessman	تاجر	ṭaajir
broker	سمسار	simsaar
doctor	دكتور/طبيب	dukṭoor/ṭabeeb
dentist	طبيب أسنان	ṭabeeb asnaan
surgeon	جرّاح	jarraah
nurse	ممرّضة	mumarriḍa

VEGETABLES AND FRUITS

vegetable	خضراء	ḳhuḍraa
potato	بطاطس	baṭaaṭis
tomato	طماطم	ṭamaaṭim

ground-nut	فول سوداني	fool soodaanee
beet	سلق	sílq
beetroot	شمندر	shammandar
chick – peas	حمص	ḥummus
beans	فول/فاصوليا	fool/faasoolyaa
seeds	بذور	badoor
pepper	فلفل	filfil
green pepper	فلفل أخضر	filfil akhdar
pomegranates	رمّان	rummaan
grapes	عنب	inab
apricots	مشمش	mishmish
almond	لوز	looz
coconuts	جوز هند	jooz hind
lemon	ليمون	lamoon
sweet lemon	ليمون حلو	lamoon ḥilw
apple	تفّاح	ṭiffaah
banana	موز	mooz
orange	برتقال	burṭuqaal
pineapple	أناناس	anaanaas
watermelon	بطّيخ	baṭṭeekh
dates	بلح/تمر	balah/ṭamir
figs	تين	ṭeen
guava	جوافة	jawaafa

onion	بصل	basal
garlic	ثوم	ṭoom
carrot	جزر	jazar
raddish	فجل	fijl
squash	قرع	qu'ra
marrows	كوسا	kawsaa
cucumber	خيار	ḳhiyaar
cauliflower	قرنبيط	qaranbeeṭ
cabbages	قرنب ملفوف	karamb malfoof

LUNCH & DINNER

vegetarian	نباتي	nabaaṭee
non vegetarian	غير نباتي	ghiar nabaaṭee
lunch	غداء	ghaḍaa
dinner	عشاء	ashaa
roasted chicken	دجاجة مشوية	ḍajaaja mashwiya
fish	سمك	samak
fried fish	سمك مقلي	samak maqlee
lobster	كركند	karkanḍ
soup	شوربة	shoorba(shoorbit)
vegetable soup	شوربة خضراء	shoorbiṭ ḳhuḍraa
mutton soup	شوربة لحم	shoorbiṭ laḥam
lentil soup	شوربة عدس	shorbiṭ adas
tomato soup	شوربة طماطم	shoorbiṭ ṭamaaṭim

COLOURS

green	أخضر/خضراء	aḳhdar/ḳhaḍraa
brown	أسمر/سمراء	asmar/samraa
pink	وردي	warḍee
orange	برتقالي	burtuqaalee
purple	أرجواني	urjuwannee
sky blue	سماوي	samaawee
grey	رمادي	rimaaḍee
white	أبيض/بيضاء	abyaḍ/bayḍaa
black	أسود/سوداء	aswaḍ/sawḍaa
yellow	أصفر/صفراء	asfar/safraa
blue	أزرق/زرقاء	aḍraq/ḍarqaa
red	أحمر/حمراء	aḥmar/ḥamraa
golden	ذهبي	ḍahabee
silver	فضّي	fiḍḍee
coffee	بُنّي	buṇṇee
violet	بنفسجي	banafsajee
scarlet	قرمزي	qirmizee
dark	غامق/عميق	ghaamiq /'ameeq
fast	ثابت	ṭaabiṭ

The colour of my dog is black.
laum kalbee aswaḍ.

لون كلبي أسود.

You are wearing
orange/purple/sky blue socks.
anṭ ṭalbis jiraabaaṭ
burṭuqaalee/urjuwaanee
samaawee.

أنت تلبس جرابات برتقالي/
أرجواني/سماوي.

I want a grey blanket.
ureeḍ burnus rimaaḍee.

أريد برنس رمادي

Do you have pink handkerchiefs?
hal inḍakum manaaḍeel warḍee?

هل عندكم مناديل
وردي؟

I want to buy brown shoes for
myself.
anaa ureeḍ ashṭaree ḥiḍaa
asmar linafsee.

أنا أريد أشتري حذاء أسمر
لنفسي

This shirt is red/white/black.
haaḍal qamees aḥmar/abyaḍ/aswaḍ.

هذا القميص أحمر/أبيض/
أسود.

My car is green/blue/yellow.
sayyaaraṭee khaḍraa/ḍarqaa/safraa.

سيّارتي خضراء/زرقاء/
صفراء.

CONVERSATION

GREETINGS

Good morning	صباح الخير	sabaaḥilḳheer
Good morning (reply)	صباح النّور	sabaaḥinnoor
Good evening	مساء الخير	masaailḳheer
Good evening (reply)	مساء النّور	masaainnoor
Good day	نهارك سعيد	nahaarak saeeḍ
Good night	ليلة سعيدة	leelaa saeeḍaa
Good bye	مع السلامة	ma'assalaamaa
See you later	إلى اللقاء	ilalliqaa
Welcome	أهلاً و سهلاً	ahlan wa sahlan
How are you?	كيف حالك ؟	keef ḥaalak
Verv well	بخير	biḳheer
Pleased to see you	سعيد لرؤيك	saeeḍ lirooyaak
I am glad	أنا فرحان	anaa farḥaan
Happy new year	عام جديد سعيد،	aam jaḍeeḍ saeeḍ
Happy Journey	رحلة سعيدة	riḥlaa saeeḍaa
Happy birthday	عيد ميلاد سعيد	eeḍmeelaaḍ saeeḍ
Congratulations	تهنياتي	tabreekaaṭ

I thank you	مشكور	mashkoor
I am grateful	أنا ممنون	anaa mamnoon
That's all right	عفوًا	'afwan
Don't mention it	لا بأس	laa baas

REQUESTS

Please (mas.)	من فضلك	min faḍlak
Please (fem.)	من فضلِك	min faḍlik
Excuse me	إسمح لي	ismaḥ lee
Please come. (mas.)	إتفضّل	iṭfaḍḍal
Please come. (fem.)	إتفضّلي	iṭfaḍḍalee
Please listen	إسمع من فضلك	ism'a min faḍlak
Please ...... slowly	على مهلك من فضلك	alaa mahlak min faḍlak
Please give me.....	أعطيني... من فضلك	aatinee.......min faḍlak
Please bring me.....	هات لي.... من فضلك	haatilee-......min fadlak
Please be quick	بسرعة من فضلك	bisuraa min faḍlak

REGRETS

Sorry	آسف / متأسف	assif/mutaasif
I am sorry	أنا آسف	anaa aasif
Sorry, I am busy	آسف! أنا مشغول	aasif anaa mashghool
Sorry, I cannot do it	آسف! أنا لا أقدر	aasif anaa laa aqḍar

ORDERS

Come	تعال	**ṭa’aal**
Go	إذهب/رُح	**iḍhab/ruḥ**
Come here.	تعال هنا	ṭa’aal hinaa
Go there.	رُح هناك/ إذهب هناك	ruḥ hunaak/ iḍhab hunaak
Go away/Get out.	رُح من هنا	ruḥ min hinaa
Give me	جب لي	jiblee
Bring me	هات لي	haatilee
Take/Take me to	خذ/خذني إلى	ḳhud/ḳhudnee ilaa
Tell	قل	qul
Speak.	تكلم	ṭakallam
Shut up	أُسكت	uskut
Call him.	نادي	naadee
Get up.	قم	qum
Come tomorrow.	تعال بكرة	ṭa’aal buḳraa
Come to my house	تعال إلى بيتي	ṭa’aal ilaa bayṭee
Look here.	شف هنا	shuf hinaa
Tell me.	قل لي	qullee
Listen to me.	إسمع ني	isma’nee
Tell him.	قل له	qullahoo

Open for me	إفتح لي	iftaḥlee
Call for me (taxi)	أُطلب لي (تاكسي)	uṭlublee (ṭaaksee)
Don't come.	لاتجئ	laa ṭajee
Don't go.	لاتذهب لاتروح.	laa ṭadhab/laa ṭaruḥ
Don't speak.	لاتتكلّم	laa ṭaṭakallam
Don't speak about me.	لاتتكلّم عنّي	laa ṭaṭakallam 'annee
Don't tell	لاتقل	laa ṭaqul
Don't tell him.	لاتقل له	laa ṭaqul lahoo
Don t play.	لاتلعب	laa ṭal'ab
Don't go to sleep.	لاتنام	laa ṭanam
Don't get afraid.	لاتخف	laa ṭakhaf
Don't forget.	لاتنسى	laa ṭansaa
Don't interrupt me.	لاتقطع كلامي	laa ṭaqṭ'a kalaamee
Don't be late.	لاتأخّر	laa ṭaakhkhar

HOW TO ASK

Is/Are/Does/Do.....?
hal......

هل......

Are you a teacher?
hal anṭ muallim?

هل أنت مدرّس؟

Is/Are/Does/Do.....?
a.........

أ......

What?
...eeh ?

إيه؟

What is your name?
ismak eeh?

إسمك إيه؟

What do you want (to have)?
taḥib eeh?

تحبّ إيه؟

Is this a hospital ?
a haadaa mustashfaa?

أهذا مستشفى؟

What.........?
maa ?

ما؟

What is your name ?
maaismak (masmak)?

ما إسمك؟ (مسمك؟)

Which ?
ayy ?

أيّ؟

Which book are you reading?
ayy kiṭaab taqraa?

أيّ كتاب تقرأ؟

Where...
ayn...

أين ...

Where is Mahmood's house?
ayn beeṭ maḥmood?

أين بيت محمود؟

What is there in your hand?
shoo fee yadik?

شو في يدك؟

'How? كيف ؟......

keef...?

How are you? كيف الحال ؟

keef alḥaal?

How much/How many ? كم ؟ ......چم ؟

kam.../cham...

What advantage is there in this? ما فائدة في هذا ؟

maa faaidaa fee haaḍaa?

What? شوُ ؟

shoo?

What is your name? شو إسمك ؟ (شسمك ؟)

shoo ismak (shusmak)?

From where? من أين ؟

minayn?

Where are you coming from? من أين تقدم ؟

minayn ṭaqḍim?

Where? وِين ؟

ween ?

Where is the airport? المطار وين ؟

almaṭaar ween?

When will you go there? متى تذهب هناك ؟

maṭaa ṭaḍhab hunaak?

Who ?

meen....?

مين؟ .....

Who are you?

meen anṭ?

مين أنت ؟

Who is in the room?

meen filḥujraa?

مين في الحجرة ؟

When?

maṭaa....?

متى؟ .....

A SIMPLE CONVERSATION

Hullo !

assalaam alaikum

ألسلام عليكم

Hullo !

alaikum assalaam wa rahms

عليكم السلام و رحمة

Good morning

sabaaḥil kheer

صباح الخير

Good morning

sabaahin noor

صباح النّور

Good evening

masail kheer

مساء الخير

Good evening

maᶜaam noor

مساء النّور

Good day. taaba yaumakum/nahaarak saeeḍ	طاب يومكم/نهارك سعيد.
Good day. ṭaaba yaumakum mubaarak/nahaarak saeeḍ mubaarak	طاب يومكم مبارك/ نهارك سعيد مبارك.
Good night. ṭaabaṭ lailatkum/laila saeeḍa	طابت ليلتكم/ ليلة سعيده.
Good night. ṭaabaṭ lailaṭkum mubaarak/laila saeeḍa mubaarak	طابت ليلتكم مبارك/ ليلة سعيدة مبارك.
Good bye. ma'assalaama/fi amaanillah	مع السلامة/ في أمان الله.
Please come. iṭfaḍḍal (mas)/iṭfaḍḍalee (fem.)	إتفضّل/ إتفضّلي.
Welcome. ahlan wa sahlan	أهلاً وسهلاً.
Thank you very much. shokran jazeelan	شكراً جزيلاً.
I am thankful. anaa mashkoor	أنا مشكور.
How are you? kaifal ḥaal/kaif ḥaalak?	كيف الحال/كيف حالك؟

Well/fine.
bikheer/ṭaiyib

بخير / طيب.

Pleased to meet you.
saeeḍ liru'yaakum

سعيد لرؤيك.

I am pleased, too.
anaa farḥaan

أنا فرحان

Where are you from?
min ain antum?

من أين أنتم؟

I am from India.
anaa minal hinḍ

أنا من الهند.

I am from Bombay.
anaa min bombaayi

أنا من بومباي.

Where were you?
ain kontum?

أين كنتم؟

I was in Kuwait.
konṭ fil kuwaiṭ

كنتُ في الكويت.

Where are you going?
ain taḍhaboon/ain ḍaahib?

أين تذهبون / أين ذاهب؟

I am going to Dubai.
aḍhab ila dubai/anaa
ḍaahib ila dubai

أذهب إلى دبئ / أنا
ذاهب إلى دبئ.

I wish you well.
aṭamannaa lakum alkheer

أتمنّى لكم الخير.

Thank you very much/I am very thankful.
shokran jiḍḍan/mashkoor waaiḍ.

شكرًا جدًّا / مشكور وائد.

MEETING OF TWO FRIENDS

Good morning Ahmed.
sabaaḥil ḳheer yaa aḥmad

صباح الخير يا أحمد

Good morning Maḥmood.
sabaaḥin noor yaa maḥmooḍ

صباح النّور يا محمود

Please come.
iṭfaḍḍal

إتفضّل!

Thank you.
shokran

شكرًا!

How are you?
kaif ḥaalakum?

كيف حالكم؟

Fine, thank you.
taiyib, mashkoor

طيّب، مشكور

I did not see you for long. Where were you?
lam arkum munḍ muḍḍa ṭaweela, ain konṭum?

لم أركم منذ مدة طويلة، أين كنتم؟

I was ill for two weeks.
konṭ mareeḍan muḍḍa osbueen

كنت مريضًا مدة أُسبوعين.

I am sorry to hear that. How are you now.?
aasif ụsimaa ̧haaḍa, .kaif anṭum alaan

آسف لسماع هذا، كيف أنتم الآن ؟

I am better today.
anaa aḥsan alyoom

أنا أحسن أليوم.

What did the doctor say ?
maadaa qaal attabeeb ?

ماذا قال الطبيب ؟

He said it was typhoid.
qaal annahoo typhoid

قال أنه تيفوئد.

I am happy that you are o.k.now
yasurrari annakum bikheer alaan.

يسرّني أنكم بخير الآن

Thank you
shokran

شكرًا!

Will you have tea ?
atatlub ashshay ?

أتطلب الشاي ؟

Please give me coffee.
min fadlik haatili qahwa

من فضلك هات لي قهوة.

Where will we go ?
ain sanadhab ?

أين سنذهب ؟

Do you know swimming ?
attaarif tasbah ?

أتعرف تسبح ؟

Not well.
laisa hasanan

ليس حسنًا.

I will come to your house tomorrow
saqdim gadan ila beetikum

ساقدم غداً إلى بيتك.

At what time ?
li ayyai saair

في أيّة ساعة ؟

At one o' clock in the afternoon.
lissaalal alwaahida
baadazzohr

في الساعة الواحدة
بعد الظهر.

Then we will go to the mountains
fanadhab ilaljabal

فنذهب إلى الجبل.

Very well, we shall go.
hasanan sanadhab

حسنًا، سنذهب.

TRAVEL

How far is it to the airport?
mal masaafaṭ ilal maṭaar?

ما المسافة إلى المطار ؟

Take me to the harbour(port).
ḳhuḍnee ilal meenaa

خذني إلى الميناء.

How much is the fare?
alujra kam/kamil ṭaman ?

الأجرة كم ؟/كم الثمن ؟

I want to get down here.
ureeḍ anzil hinaa

أريد أنزل هنا.

Please take the luggage down.
nazzil alamṭia min faḍlak

نزّل الأمتعة من فضلك

Do not delay/Do not be late.
laa ṭaaḳhḳhir

لا تأخّر

Please call me a taxi. أطلب لي تاكسي من فضلك.
uṭlub lee ṭaaksee min faḍlak

What is the fare to the station? كم الأجرة إلى المحطّة ؟
kam ilujra ilal maḥaṭṭa?

What is the charge per day? كم الثمن ليوم ؟
kam ilṭaman liyoom?

Where can I get a taxi? أين أجد تاكسي ؟
ain ajiḍ ṭaaksee?

Is this seat reserved? الكرسي هذا محجوز ؟
alkursee ḥaaḍa maḥjooz?

Please open the window إفتح الشبّاك من فضلك.
ifṭah ashshubbaak min faḍlak

Where can I get a ticket? أين أجد التذكرة ؟
ain ajiḍ aṭṭaḍkara?

Ḥow long does the journey take? ما مدة الرّحلة ؟
maa muḍḍaṭ arriḥla?

What time do we arrive? متى نصل ؟
maṭaa nasil?

What time does the plane take off? متى تقوم الطائرة ؟
maṭaa ṭaqoom attaaira?

What is the flight number? ما نمرة الرحلة ؟
maa nimriṭ arrihla?

I think this is my seat أظنّ أن هذا الكرسي لي.
azun an haaḍal kursee lee

How do I reach the hotel? كيف أصل إلى الفندق ؟
kaif asil ilal funḍuq?

Is there a bus available in the town? هل يوجد باص في البلد ؟
hal yoojaḍ bus fil balaḍ?

Is the hotel far away from here? هل الفندق بعيد من هنا ؟
hal alfunḍuq baeeḍ min hinaa?

No, not so far. كلا ، ليس بعيدًا جدًّا .
kalla laisa baeeḍan jiḍḍan

Is the train late? هل القطار متأخّر ؟
halil qiṭaar muṭaakhkhar?

Where is the passport office? أين ادارة الجوازات ؟
ain iḍaaraṭ aljawaazaaṭ?

Do you have a passport? هل عندك جواز السفر ؟
hal inḍak jawaaz assafar?

Yes, I have a passport. نعم عندي جواز السفر
na'am inḍi jawaaz assafar موجود .
mawjooḍ

I want an entry permit. (أنا) أريد تصريح الدخول
(anaa) oreed ṭasreeh aḍḍukhool

Will you travel by sea or by air? هل تسافر بحرًا أو جوًّا ؟
hal ṭusaafir bahran aw
jawwan?

I will travel by air. إنّي أسافر جوًّا .
inni usaafir jawwan

Have you ever travelled to Arab land?
hal saafarṭa yawman ilalarab?

هل سافرت يومًا إلى العرب؟

I have travelled to Abu-Dhabi once.
saafarṭu marraṭan ila abuḍhahbi

سافرتُ مرّتين إلى أبوظهبي.

Why do you want to travel to Kuwait?
limaaḍa ṭusaafir ilalkuwaiṭ?

لماذا تسافر إلى الكويت؟

To serve
lilisṭikhdaam

للإستخدام.

For business
liṭṭijaara

للتجارة

Do you have anything to declare (forbidden)?
hal inḍak amṭia mın almamnooa?

هل عندك أمتعة من الممنوعة؟

I have nothing to declare.
laisa inḍi shay o'lan anhu

ليس عندي شيء أعلن عنه.

I have a tape recorder.
inḍi aalaṭ aṭṭasjeel

عندي آلة التسجيل.

Where is your luggage?
ain amṭıaṭak?

اين أمتعتك ؟

Please open it.
iftah haaḍihi min faḍlak

إفتح هذه من فضلك.

With pleasure, sir.
bikul suroor yaa seeḍee

بكلّ سرور ياسيدي.

Is this bag yours?
hal haaḍihi shunṭa lak?

هل هذه شنطة لك ؟

Do you have anything to pay duty for ?
hal ma'ak shay litadfa alaihi jumruk ?

هل معك شئ لتدفع عليه جمرك ؟

I have a carton of cigarettes/a bottle of whisky.
inḍi kharṭooshaṭ sajaair/ zujaaja viski

عندي خرطوشة سجائر/ زجاجة وسكي.

Must I pay for this?
hal yajib an aḍfa an haaḍa

هل يجب أن أدفع عن هذا؟

No, sir!
laa yaa seeḍee

لا ياسيدي.

This is a watch for my personal use.
innahaa assaa'a liisti maali alshakhsi

إنّها الساعة لإستعمال الشخصي.

It is a used one.
innahaa musta'mala

إنّها مستعملة.

Do you have any more luggage ?
hal indak amita ukhraa ?

هل عندك أمتعة أخرى ؟

You will have to pay penalty. | لازم تدفع غرامة.
laazim ṭaḍfa gharaama

Nothing at all | لا شئ ابداً.
laa shay abadan

I have only my clothes. | معي ملابسي فقط
maee malaabisi faqat.

No, sir | لا يا سيدي
laa yaa seedee

Where is the travelling agency? | وكالة السفريات وين؟
wakaalaṭ assafariyaaṭ ween?

Any service, sir? | أية خدمة يا سيدي؟
aiya ḳhidma ya seeḍee?

I want a ticket for Dubai. | أريد تذكرة لدبئ.
oreeḍ ṭaḍkira liḍubai

What is your full name? | شسمك كامل؟
shusmak kaamil?

What is there in this box (trunk)? | أيش في صندوق هذا؟
aish fisandooq haaḍa?

There are gifts for my kids. | هدايا لأولادي.
haḍaaya liawlaaḍi

IN THE CITY

Where is the post office, please? | مكتب البريد وين من فضلك؟
makṭabil bareeḍ ween min faḍlak?

What is the name of your hotel? shoo ism ooṭeelak?	شو اسم أوتيلك ؟
The name of my hotel is Sheraton. ism ooṭeelee Sheratoon	إسم أوتيلي شيراتون
Where is the nearest hospital? aqrab mustashfaa ween?	أقرب مستشفى وين ؟
The nearest hospital is near the station. aqrab mustashfaa inḍ mahaṭṭa	أقرب مستشفى عند محطّة.
Where is the market, sir? assooq ween yaa seedee?	السوق وين يا سيدي ؟
The way to the market is from this side. assooq min hinaa	السوق من هنا.
Where do I get a bus? ain yoojaḍ albaas?	أن يوجد الباص ؟
Is there any English speaking person? hal yoojaḍ rajul yaṭakallam injliziyya?	هل يوجد رجل يتكلّم إنجليزية؟
What building is this? maa haaḍa almabnaa?	ما هذا المبنى؟
I want to see it. ureeḍ an araahaa	أريد أن أراها.
Can we go together? anaḍhab sawiyyan?	أنذهب سويًا؟

Which restaurant do we go to?
shoo maṭaam naḍhab?

شو مطعم نذهب؟

Do you ḥave a room or flat to let?
hal inḍakum hujra aw shaqqa lilijaara?

هل عندكم حجرة أو شقة للإجارة؟

I want one room or flat on third floor.
ureeḍ waaḥidaṭan fiṭṭaabiq aṭṭaaliṭ

أريد واحدةً في الطابق الثالث

Do you want it furnished?
aṭareedahaa mafroosha?

أتريدها مفروشة؟

What is the rent?
kamil eejar?

كم الايجار؟

Which bus goes to Muscat?
ayy baas ṭaḍhab ilaa masqaṭ?

أيّ باص تذهب إلى مسقط؟

When is the next train to Damascus?
maṭaa yaqoom alqiṭaar alqaaḍim ilaa dimishq?

متى يقوم القطار القادم إلى دمشق؟

How much is the fare?
bikam aṭṭaḍkara

بكم التذكرة؟

IN THE RESTAURANT

Welcome, Sir!
ahlan wa sahlan yaa seeḍee

أهلاً وسهلاً يا سيدي

Where would you like to sit?
ain ṭureeḍ an ṭajlis?

أين تريد أن تجلس؟

We shall all sit there at the corner. (sanajlis)hunaak fizzaawiyaa	سنجلس هناك في الزاوية.
Menu, Please! qaaimaṭaṭ ṭa'aam min faḍlak	قائمة الطعام من فضلك.
With great pleasure. bikul suroor yaa seeḍee	بكُل سُرور يا سيدي.
What would you like(to have)? ṭaḥib shoo/maa ṭureeḍ?	تحب شو/ ما ترُيد؟
I want to have omelette/soup/fruit juice. -ureeḍ ijja/shoorba/aseer faakihaa	أريد عجّة/شوربة/ عصير فاكهة.
Please give me bread/sugar/more butter. -aaṭini ḳhubz/sukkar/zib-ḍaa/ziyaada min faḍlak	أعطني خبز/ سكرّ/ زبدة/ زيادة من فضلك.
I want egg and rice. anaa aawiz beed wa ruz	أنا عاوز بيض و رُز
I will have tea/coffee. anaa ashrib shaay/qahwa	أنا أشرب شاي/قهوة
May I have the bill please. ureeḍ alḥisaab minfaḍlak	أريد الحساب من فضلك.
That's not what I ordered. haaḍaa lais maa ṭalabṭoo	هذا ليس ما طلبتُ.
It cannot be cnanged. laa yumkin ṭaghyeer haaḍaa	لا يمكن تغيير هذا.
Keep the change. iḥṭafiẓ bilbaaqee	إحتفظ بالباقي.

HOTELS AND ROOMS

I want to stay in a hotel.
ureeḍ iqaama fiuṭeel
أريد إقامة في أوتيل

I have a reservation.
inḍee ḥajaz
عندي حجز

My name is...
ismee...
إسمي ....

How is your hotel?
keef uṭeelak
كيف أوتيلك ؟

Our service is very good.
ḳhiḍmatunaa ṭayyiba jiḍḍan
خدمتنا طيّبة جدّاً.

I want a single/
airconditioned room.
ureeḍ ghurfa
lishaḳhs/ghurfa mukayyafa.
أريد غرفة لشخص/
غرفة مكيّفة.

I want a double room/
a room with bath.
ureeḍ ghurfa lishkh-
sain/ghurfa lahaa ḥammaam
أريد غرفة لشخصين/
غرفة لها حمام.

How much is the charge
per day/per week?
kamil ajr
lilyoom/limuḍḍaṭusboo?.
كم أجر لليوم ؟/لمدة
أسبوع ؟

Do you want it
for a week / a month?
aṭureeḍahaa
liusbu/lishahr?
أتريدها لأسبوع/
لشهر؟

Yes. Do you want a furnished one? نعم، أتريدها مفروشة ؟
naam aṭureeḍuha mafroosha?

Yes, a furnished one on the third floor/in the front/ at the back. نعم، مفروشة وفي الطابق الثالث/في الأمام/ في الخلف.

na'am mafrosha wa fiṭ-ṭaabiq aṭṭaaliṭ filamaam/filkhalf.

This room is too small for us. هذه الغرفة صغيرة لنا.
haaḍihil ghurfa sagheera lanaa.

We want a flat/suite. نريد شقه.
nureeḍ shaqqa.

That is on the fourth floor. إنّها في الطابق الرابع .
innahaa fiṭaabiq arraabi.

Let me/us see it. دعني أراها/دعنا نراها.
ḍa'anee araahaa da'anaa naraaha.

What is the rent? كم الإيجار/كم الثمن ؟
kamileejaar/kamil ṭaman?

What is the number of my key/room? ماهو نمرة (رقم) مفتاحي/ غرفتي ؟

maa huwaa nimraṭ (ra-qam) mifṭaahee/ghurfaṭee?

Is a telephone available here? هل يوجد هاتف ؟
hal yoojad haaṭif?

Please get me soap/towel/blanket. من فضلك، إحضرلي صابون/مِنشف/بُرنس.
min faḍlak iḥḍarlee saa-boon/minshaf/burnus.

AT THE POST-OFFICE

Where is the post office? maktabil bareed ween?	مكتب البريد وين؟
It is far off/ close by ? huwa baeed/qareeb min hinaa?	هو بعيد/قريب من هنا.
I want to send this letter. ureed an arsal haadal maktoob	أريد أن أرسل هذا المكتوب.
I want to receive my parcel. ureed an astalim tardee	أريد أن أستلم طردي.
Is there a money order for me? hal hawaala bareediyya lee	هل حوالة بريدية لي؟
There is none. maa fee	ما في.
Where is the stamp window? shubbaak tawaabi ween?	شبّاك طوابع وين؟
Please give me stamps/envelopes. aatinee tawaabi/zuroof min fadlak	أعطيني طوابع/ظروف من فضلك.
From where can I send a telegram? ainyumkin an arsal barqiyya?	أين يمكن أن أرسل برقية؟

IN A GARMENTS SHOP

I want a silk shirt. ureed qamees hareer	أيّة خدمة يا سيد
How do you like this one? kaif tajid haadaa?	أريد قميص حرير.

This is a beautiful shirt.
innahu qamees jameel

إنّه قميص جميل.

But it is tight.
wa laakin haaḍaa ḍayyaq

ولكن هذا ضيّق.

This blue suit is very beautiful.
haaḍihil baḍla alazraq jameela jiḍḍan

هذه البدلة الأزرق جميلة جدًّا.

This is the best quality.
haaḍaa afḍal sinf

هذا أفضل صنف؟

What is the price?
maa ṭaman?

ما ثمن؟

I want to buy some cloth.
ureeḍ an ashṭaree qimaashan

أريد أن أشتري قماشًا.

What do you want it for?
limaaḍaa tureeḍ?

لماذا تريد؟

I want it for a night dress.
ureeḍ limalboos nawm

أريد لملبوس نوم.

What size do you wear?
ay ḥajam ṭalbis?

أيّ حجم تلبس؟

I don't know very well.
laa aalam ṭamaaman

لا أعلم تمامًا.

Please take the measurement.
qiss min faḍlak

قسّ من فضلك.

Which colour do you want?
ay lawn ṭareeḍ?

أيّ لون تريد؟

I want black pants.
ureeḍ banṭaloon aswaḍ

أريد بنطلون أسود.

Do you have good handkerchiefs ?
hal inḍakum manaaḍeel zain?

هل عندكم مناديل زين؟

THE HOUSE

My house is at Muhammed Ali Road.
manzilee alaa shaari muḥammeḍ alee.

منزلي على شارع محمد علي.

There is a lift in my building.
hunaak mus'iḍ fi manzilee.

هناك مصعد في منزلي.

Who lives on the floor above(you)?
man saakin alaa ṭaabiq fauq?

من ساكن على طابق فوق ؟

How do you like my house?
maa raayuk fi manzilee?.

ما رأيك في منزلي ؟

It is very nice,
and its location is also good
aẓeem wa mauqahu munaasib aiḍan.

عظيم ! وموقعه مناسب أيضًا.

Is there a balcony?
ahunaak shurfa

أهناك شرفة ؟

The furniture is new.
almafrooshaaṭ jaḍeeḍa.

المفروشات جديدة.

The lift is not working.
almus'iḍ lais fil amal.

المصعد ليس في العمل.

Your bed is very comfortable.
sareerakum mareeḥ

سريركم مريح.

RELATIONS

My son is married
ibnee muṭazawwaj.

إبني متزوج.

My sister is a divorcee
ukhṭee muṭallaqa.

اختي مطلّقة.

Is your father in Bombay?
hal abook fi bumbaayee

هل أبوك في بومباي؟

No, he is in Kuwait
laa huwaa fil kuwayṭ.

لا، هو في الكويت.

Where is your son/daughter?
ibnak/ibnaṭak ween.

إبنك/إبنتك وين؟

He/she lives in Abu Dhabi
huwaa/hiyaa yaskun/ṭaskun
fi abu ḍhahabi.

هو/هي يسكن/تسكن في أبوظبي.

Your wife/daughter is beautiful
zawjaṭak/binṭak jameela.

زوجتك/بنتك جميلة.

STAGES OF LIFE

This young man is a bachelor.
haaḍa ashshaab aanis.

هذا الشاب آنس.

The boy/girl is going to school.
aṭṭifl/aṭṭiflaa yaḍhab/ṭaḍhab
ilalmaḍrasaa.

الطفل/الطفلة يذهب/تذهب إلى المدرسة.

The man/the woman is married.
arrajul muṭzawwaj/alimra muṭ-
zawwajaa

الرجل متزوّج/الإمراة متزوّجة

Where is your bride?
aroosak ween.?

عروسك وين؟

Do not waste your youth.
laa ṭaḍee ashshabaab.

لاتضيع الشباب

HOW TO TELL THE TIME

What is the time? كم الساعة ؟
kamissaa'aa

Would you mind telling me
the time, please? الساعة كم من فضلك ؟
assaa'aa kam min faḍlak.

At what time does the shop
open/close? متى يفتح/يقبل الدكان ؟
maṭaa yaftaḥ/yaqbal aḍ ḍukaan?

At what time the film will
start/end? متى يبدأ/ينتهي الفيلم ؟
maṭaa yabḍaa/yanṭahee alfeelam?

HEALTH

What is your complaint? ماذا بك ؟
maadaa bik?

I have a severe headache. عندي وجع رأس شديد.
inḍee waj'a rass shaḍeeḍ.

You have caught a cold. أخذت بردًا
aḳhaḍṭa barḍan.

Yes, and a cough too. نعم، وسعال أيضًا.
na'am wa suaal aiḍan.

How do you feel now? ماذا تشعر الآن ؟
maaḍaa tash'ur alaan.

I am feeling dizzy. أنا دائخ.
anaa ḍaaiḳh.

Your pulse is racing. نبضكم سريع.
nabḍukum sareeun.

Her husband/his wife is young
zaujahaa/zaujaṭahu
shaab/shaaba .

زوجها/زوجته شابّ/شابّة.

You go with your brother/sister
anṭa iḍhab ma'a aḳhak/uḳhṭak.

إنت إذهب مع أخك/أختك.

Your father in law/son in law is an officer
hamook/ sihrak daabiṭ

حموك/سهرك ضابط.

My brother/sister is married
aḳhee/uḳhṭee muṭzawwaj/muṭzawwaja

أخي/ أختي متزوج/ متزوجة.

Please call the doctor.
uṭlub ṭabeeb(ḍukṭoor) min faḍlak.

أطلب طبيب (دكتور) من فضلك

Take these pills/medicines.
ḳhuḍ haadihee huboob/aḍwiyaa.

خذ هذه حبوب/ادوية

Vocabulary

The words in brackets are the customary plurals which are all feminine. Five of the commonest plurals are indicated by letters:

أَفْعَالٌ a — فُعُولٌ b — فِعَالٌ c — فُعُلٌ d — أَفْعُلٌ e

نَهْرٌ (أَنْهَارٌ) river, canal.

مَلِكٌ (مُلُوكٌ) king.

بُسْتَانٌ (بَسَاتِينُ) garden.

خُبْزٌ bread.

شَارِعٌ (شَوَارِعُ) street.

إِنْسَانٌ (نَاسٌ) human being.

كَبِيرٌ big.

نَظِيفٌ clean.

فَقِيرٌ poor.

حَسَنٌ good, beautiful.

عَرِيضٌ wide.

وَاسِعٌ spacious.

طَيِّبٌ good. لَطِيفٌ gracious.

كِتَابٌ (d) book.

ظِلٌّ (c) shade, shadow.

خَفِيفٌ light.

كَرِيمٌ noble, generous.

مَفْتُوحٌ opened, open.

شُبَّاكٌ (شَبَابِيكُ) window.

بَيْتٌ (بُيُوتٌ) house.

بَحْرٌ (بِحَارٌ) sea.

رَجُلٌ (رِجَالٌ) man.

لَحْمٌ flesh, meat.

قَصْرٌ (قُصُورٌ) castle, palace.

وَلَدٌ (أَوْلَادٌ) child, boy.

صَغِيرٌ little.

وَسِخٌ dirty.

غَنِيٌّ rich.

قَبِيحٌ ugly, bad.

حَبِيبٌ beloved, friend.

صَادِقٌ truthful.

قَدِيمٌ old (of things).

طَرِيقٌ (d) road.

سَلَامَةٌ safety.

رَأْسٌ (b) head.

مَخَافَةٌ fear.

صَحْنٌ (b) courtyard, dish.

شَعْرٌ (a) hair.

قِطْعَةٌ (قِطَعٌ) piece.

خَادِمٌ (خُدَّامٌ) servant.

نَجَّارٌ carpenter.

فَرَّاشٌ domestic servant.

خَيَّاطَةٌ sempstress.

حُجْرَةٌ (حُجَرٌ) room.

فَرَسٌ (a) horse, mare.

لَاعِبٌ playing (participle).

جَالِسٌ sitting.

مُظِلٌّ giving shade, shady.

قَرَّ i. قَرَارٌ be firm, fixed.

دَلَّ u. دَلٌّ guide.

إِقَاءٌ (inf. of لَقِيَ) meeting.

وَطَنٌ (a) native land.

شَاعِرٌ (شُعَرَاءُ) poet.

وَزْنٌ (a) weight.

سَرِيعٌ swift.

شَرَفٌ honour.

لَبَنٌ (a) milk.

ضَعِيفٌ weak.

جَمَلٌ (c) male camel.

نَاقَةٌ (نُوقٌ) female camel.

مَعْزٌ goats.

ثَوْرٌ (ثِيرَانٌ) bull.

زَيْتُونٌ olives, olive trees.

زَيْتٌ olive oil, oil.

صَاحِبٌ (a) companion, master, owner.

طَبِيبٌ (أَطِبَّاءُ) physician.

خَبَّازٌ baker.

طَبَّاخٌ cook.

خَيَّاطٌ tailor.

أُذُنٌ (a) ear.

بَقَّالٌ greengrocer.

حِمَارٌ (حَمِيرٌ) donkey.

مَشْغُولٌ busy, busied.

قَصِيرٌ short.

خَفَّ X despise.

حَبَّ IV love, like.

مَلَّ a. مَلَلٌ be disgusted with.

شِعْرٌ (a) poetry, poem.

قَوِيٌّ strong.

قُوَّةٌ (قُوًى) strength.

عَقْلٌ (b) reason, intelligence.

هِمَّةٌ (هِمَمٌ) care, anxiety.

تَجْرِبَةٌ (تَجَارِبُ) experience.

كَثْرَةٌ multitude, abundance.

مَعْلُومٌ known.

شَاةٌ (شَاءٌ) a sheep.

بَقَرٌ cattle (sing. بَقَرَةٌ).

خَيْلٌ horses, horsemen.

جَامُوسٌ (جَوَامِيسُ) buffalo.

شَغَلَ VIII work, be busy.

مَطْبَخٌ kitchen.

وَارِثٌ (وَرَثَةٌ) heir.

حَارِسٌ (حُرَّاسٌ) a guard, watchful.

دُكَّانٌ (دَكَاكِينُ) shop.

عَامٌّ general.

عَامَّةٌ (عَوَامُّ) the common herd.

حِنْطَةٌ wheat.

شَعِيرٌ barley.

صَدْرٌ (b) breast, chest.

إِصْبَعٌ (أَصَابِعُ) finger.

مِرْفَقٌ (مَرَافِقُ) elbow.

عُنُقٌ (a) neck.

سَرَقَ i. سَرَقٌ steal.

شَفَةٌ lip.

هَوَاءٌ air.

شِمَالٌ north.

شَرْقٌ — مَشْرِقٌ east.

شَهْرٌ (b — e) month.

نَهَارٌ day, daylight.

جِدَارٌ (d) wall.

قَلْبٌ (b) heart.

نَجَحَ a. نَجَاحٌ succeed.

تَبِعَ تَبَعٌ and VIII follow.

جَدَّةٌ grandmother.

قَلْبٌ (b) heart.

عَالِمٌ (عُلَمَاءُ) learned man.

عَقْرَبٌ (عَقَارِبُ) scorpion.

كَلْبٌ (c) dog.

فَلَّاحٌ peasant.

خَاصٌّ special.

خَاصَّةٌ (خَوَاصُّ) the upper ten.

قَمْحٌ wheat (ripe).

ذُرَةٌ millet, maize.

كَتِفٌ (a) shoulder.

إِبْهَامٌ (أَبَاهِيمُ) thumb.

ظُفْرٌ (a) finger nail.

بَارِدٌ cold.

جَفْنٌ (b) eyelid.

جَوْزٌ nut.

خَالٌ (a) maternal uncle.

خَالَةٌ maternal uncle.

نَوْءٌ (a) storm.

نَسِيمٌ (c) breeze.

جَنُوبٌ south.

غَرْبٌ — مَغْرِبٌ west.

دَقِيقَةٌ (دَقَائِقُ) minute.

ظَهْرٌ (b) back.

ظُهْرٌ noon.

حَمَّامٌ bath (Turkish).

قُفْلٌ (a) lock.

وَجْهٌ (b) face.

جَارٌ (جِيرَانٌ) protected alien, neighbour.

بَابٌ (a) door, chapter.

كِسَاءٌ (أَكْسِيَةٌ) clothing, covering.

مِفْتَاحٌ (مَفَاتِيحُ) key.

لِسَانٌ (أَلْسِنَةٌ) tongue.

رَفِيقٌ (رُفَقَاءُ) companion.

جَارِيَةٌ (جَوَارٍ) [1] girl.

مَدِينَةٌ (d) town.

أُمٌّ (أُمَّهَاتٌ) mother.

رِيحٌ (c) wind.

جَزِيرَةٌ (جَزَائِرُ) island.

أَرْضٌ (أَرَضُونَ) earth, land.

شَجَرٌ (a) trees.

جَدِيدٌ new.

بَعِيدٌ far, distant.

حَارٌّ hot.

طَوِيلٌ long, tall.

بِنْتٌ (بَنَاتٌ) daughter.

رِجْلٌ (e) foot, leg.

قَدَمٌ (a) foot, leg.

نَعَمْ yes.

كَثِيرٌ many, much.

جَمِيلٌ beautiful.

ثَقِيلٌ heavy.

شَرِيفٌ (a) noble.

لَا no, not.

حِفْظٌ keeping (abstract noun).

عِزٌّ might.

حِكْمَةٌ (حِكَمٌ) wisdom, wise saying.

تَاجِرٌ (تُجَّارٌ) merchant.

أُخْتٌ (أَخَوَاتٌ) sister.

دَارٌ (آدُرٌ) house.

عَجُوزٌ (عَجَائِزُ) old woman

سُوقٌ (a) market.

نَارٌ (نِيرَانٌ) fire.

شَمْسٌ sun.

شَيْخٌ (b) old man, chief.

شَدِيدٌ strong, violent.

قَرِيبٌ near.

عَزِيزٌ mighty.

نَفْسٌ (b) soul.

عَيْنٌ (b) eye.

سَاقٌ (سِيقَانٌ) leg, stalk

خَلِيفَةٌ (خُلَفَاءُ) deputy, caliph

غَنَمٌ sheep (collective).

قَلِيلٌ few.

قِصَرٌ قَصُرَ be short.

قَالَ u. قَوْلٌ say.

قَالَ i. قَيْلٌ take a siesta.

عُلُوقٌ عَلِقَ be attached to.

صَارَ i. صَيْرٌ become.

قَامَ u. قِيَامٌ stand, stand up.

عَادَ u. عَوْدٌ return.

بَاعَ i. بَيْعٌ sell.

عِدَّةٌ number.

حَدِيدٌ iron.

حُبٌّ love.

(حُجَجٌ) حُجَّةٌ argument.

(قَوَافِلُ) قَافِلَةٌ caravan.

نَظَرَ u. نَظَرٌ look at, see.

غَضَبٌ غَضِبَ be angry.

فَعَلَ a. فِعْلٌ do, act.

جَمَعَ a. جَمْعٌ collect (trans.).

سَبَحَ a. سِبَاحَةٌ swim.

عَدُوٌّ (a) enemy.

شِتَاءٌ winter.

صَفٌّ (b) row, rank.

صَنَعَ a. صُنْعٌ make, do.

جَلَسَ i. جُلُوسٌ sit.

قُدُومٌ قَدِمَ advance, arrive.

نَبَحَ a. نَبْحٌ bark.

طَبْلٌ (b) drum.

وَحْدٌ (always with a suffix) alone.

طَالَ u. طُولٌ be long.

كَانَ u. كَوْنٌ become, be.

تَرَكَ u. تَرْكٌ leave.

مَاتَ u. مَوْتٌ die.

سَارَ i. سَيْرٌ go, travel.

خَافَ a. خَوْفٌ fear.

مَالَ i. مَيْلٌ incline.

غَلَبَ i. غَلْبٌ overcome.

بُخْلٌ avarice.

حَجَرٌ (a) stone.

لُصٌّ (b) thief, brigand.

حَبْلٌ (e) rope.

جَيْشٌ (b) army.

بَلَدٌ (c) town.

كَأْسٌ (b) (fem.) cup.

(دَنَانِيرُ) دِينَارٌ dinar, gold coin (Latin denarius).

ثَوْبٌ (c) piece of cloth, clothing.

كَرَامَةٌ كَرُمَ be noble, generous

ضَحْكٌ ضَحِكَ laugh.

صَيْفٌ summer.

خَشَبٌ wood.

(بُلْدَانٌ) بِلَادٌ country.

جَمَاعَةٌ party, company.

ضَلَّ i. ضَلَالٌ go astray.

فَرَقَ u. i. فَرْقٌ separate.
غَفَرَ i. غُفْرَانٌ cover, pardon.
صَرَفَ i. صَرْفٌ turn (trans.).
نظر IV cause to wait.
قَبِلَ قَبُولٌ receive.
قبل III compare.
ضرب VIII be confused, in commotion.
زَحَمَ a. زَحْمٌ push.
ذَخَرَ a. ذُخْرٌ select.
دَرَسَ u. دَرْسٌ study.
ثَلْجٌ (b) snow.
عيدٌ (a) festival.
علم II teach.
V learn.
وجه II (turn the face) send.
وَجَدَ وُجُودٌ find.
وَقَفَ وُقُوفٌ stand.
وسع a. سعةٌ be wide, include, be able.
وجب وُجُوبٌ be necessary.
وَرِثَ i. وِرْثٌ inherit.
ودع a. وَدْعٌ leave.
وَكَلَ وَكْلٌ entrust.
وهم VIII suspect.
صِفَةٌ (صِفَاتٌ) description, quality.
هَزَمَ i. هَزْمٌ defeat.
بَلَغَ u. بُلُوغٌ arrive at.
VII turn away, go away.
VIII expect, wait for.
IV go forward.
نزع III try to take away, quarrel.
حصر III besiege.
VIII crowd.
VIII store up.
II teach.
حَاجَةٌ need, business, thing.
حِصْنٌ (b) fortress.
IV tell, make known.
غَابَ i. غُيُوبٌ be absent.
عَدْلٌ justice.
فَيْلَسُوفٌ (فلاسِفة) philosopher.
مَقْدَرَةٌ strength.
سُوءٌ evil, badness.
وجه V (send oneself) go.
وَصَلَ وُصُولٌ reach, arrive at, give.
وَصَفَ وَصْفٌ describe.
وسع VIII be wide.
وَرَدَ وُرُودٌ go down.
وَضَعَ وَضْعٌ put, put down.

صوب II think right.

حول VIII employ devices, tricks.

عَوْنٌ help.

بيع VIII buy.

صيد VIII take by hunting.

حوج VIII need, be in want (always with إِلَى).

لَوْنٌ (a) colour, course (at a meal).

زَهْرٌ (b) flower.

مُصِيبَةٌ (مَصَائِبُ) calamity.

صَلَاةٌ (صَلَوَاتٌ) prayer, the Muslim form of worship.

مَوْهَبَةٌ (مَوَاهِبُ) gift.

ذِرَاعٌ (e) forearm, arm, cubit.

تَمْرٌ dates, sing. تَمْرَةٌ.

سَرَّ u. سُرُورٌ please, delight.

حسّ IV to perceive, know.

عَدَّ u. عَدٌّ count.

مَرَّ u. مُرُورٌ pass by.

مَدَّ u. مَدٌّ stretch.

رَدَّ u. رَدٌّ come back, send back.

خَفَّ i. خِفَّةٌ be light (weight)

عَفَّ i. عِفَّةٌ be chaste, temperate.

قَصَّ u. قَصٌّ tell a story, cut.

نَصْرَانِيٌّ (نَصَارَى) Christian.

سَتَرَ u. سَتْرٌ hide.

مَا بَالُ what about, what is the matter with ?

صوب IV come upon, hit.

حِيلَةٌ (حِيَلٌ) trick, stratagem, device.

لَئِيمٌ (c) base, ignoble.

نَوْمٌ sleep.

أَسْمَرُ brown.

نَخْلٌ sing. نَخْلَةٌ palm tree.

حُمْرَةٌ redness.

زُرْقَةٌ blueness.

بَيَاضٌ whiteness.

أَخْضَرُ green, dark coloured.

أَطْرَشُ deaf.

أَخْرَسُ dumb.

حَيَّةٌ (حَيَّاتٌ) snake.

مُصْعَبٌ a man's name.

ظَنَّ u. ظَنٌّ have an opinion.

فَرَّ i. فِرَارٌ run away.

عدّ IV prepare (trans.).

عدّ X prepare oneself.

مرّ X continue.

مدّ IV help, reinforce.

مدّ X ask for help.

وَكِيلٌ (وُكَلاءُ) agent, man of business.

جَهْلٌ ignorance.

مَدْخَلٌ (مَدَاخِلُ) entrance.

فِضَّةٌ silver.

صِرَاطٌ path.

حَدِيدٌ sharp.

عَسِيرٌ difficult.

قَبِيلَةٌ (قَبَائِلُ) tribe.

قَوْلٌ (a) speech, word, what is said.

خُضْرَةٌ greenness, being a dark colour.

صُفْرَةٌ yellowness.

سَوَادٌ blackness.

أَزْرَقُ blue.

أَصْفَرُ yellow, pale.

قوم IV stay, set up.

وَعَدَ i. وَعْدٌ promise.

طوع IV obey.

طَوْعًا willingly.

عون IV help.

يَهُودُ Jews. يَهُودِيٌّ (sing.).

خُفَّاشٌ (خَفَافِيشُ) bat (animal).

بَالٌ mind.

مَنَارَةٌ (مَنَاوِرُ) lighthouse, minaret.

دَابَّةٌ (دَوَابُّ) riding animal.

قَلَمٌ (a) reed pen.

حَكِيمٌ (حُكَمَاءُ) wise man.

ذَهَبٌ gold.

مَالٌ (a) wealth, property, money.

مَخْرَجٌ (مَخَارِجُ) exit.

وَرَقٌ (a) leaf, paper.

سَيْفٌ (b) sword.

دَقِيقٌ fine, thin (lit. powdered).

يَسِيرٌ few, easy.

أَحْدَبُ hunch-backed.

حُلْوٌ sweet.

أَعْوَرُ one-eyed.

أَعْرَجُ lame.

مُرٌّ bitter, sour.

حَيَاءٌ shame, modesty.

نَقَدَ u. نَقْدٌ pay cash.

قيد VII obey.

خير VIII choose.

قوم X be straight.

وعد IV threaten.

طوع X be able.

وَعِيدٌ threat.

عون X ask the help of.

ضَرَبَ i. ضَرْبٌ hit, strike.

طَلَبَ u. طَلَبٌ seek, look for.

خَرَجَ u. خُرُوجٌ go, come out.

ذَهَبَ a. ذَهَابٌ go away.

كَسَرَ i. كَسْرٌ break.

بَعَثَ a. بَعْثٌ send.

سَمِعَ سَمْعٌ hear.

كَتَبَ u. كِتَابَةٌ write.

لَعِبَ لَعْبٌ play.

ذَكَرَ u. ذِكْرٌ remember, mention.

شَبِعَ شَبَعٌ be satisfied (with food).

كَلَامٌ speech, what is said.

جَبَلٌ (c) mountain.

فَتَلَ i. فَتْلٌ twist.

حَمَلَ i. حَمْلٌ carry.

طَعَنَ u. طَعْنٌ thrust, pierce, criticise.

حَرَمَ i. حَرِيمٌ forbid.

نَشَدَ u. نَشْدٌ seek, adjure.

صَامَ u. صَوْمٌ fast.

اَلْإِسْتَانَةُ Stamboul.

مِيتَةٌ mode of death.

عِنَايَةٌ care.

فَرْسَخٌ parasang (about three miles).

مَشْكُوكٌ doubted.

زُبْدٌ butter.

فَهِمَ فَهْمٌ understand.

فَتَحَ a. فَتْحٌ open, conquer.

دَخَلَ u. دُخُولٌ enter.

رَجَعَ i. رُجُوعٌ return.

نَزَلَ i. نُزُولٌ come down, dismount, camp.

شَرِبَ شَرْبٌ drink.

قَطَعَ a. قَطْعٌ cut, cut off.

حَفِظَ حَفْظٌ keep, guard.

صَعِدَ صُعُودٌ go up.

صَرَخَ u. صُرَاخٌ cry for help.

صَوْتٌ (a) voice, noise.

لَبَنٌ (a) milk.

قَرَّ u. قُرٌّ be cold.

خبر IV tell, report.

II put a burden on, load.

حَرُمَ حَرَامٌ be unlawful, tabu.

نشد IV recite (poetry).

لام u. لَوْمٌ blame.

ضَاقَ i. ضِيقٌ be narrow.

رِفْقٌ kindness.

هَنْدَسَةٌ engineering.

سِكَّةٌ (سِكَكٌ) coin, road.

نَسَبٌ (a) pedigree, family honour.

تَمْرٌ dates (coll.) تَمْرَةٌ a date.

رَمَضَانُ ninth month of Muslim year.

قرأ a. قِرَاءَةٌ read, repeat.

أَسِيرٌ (أَسْرَى) prisoner.

دِينٌ (a) religion.

حَسَدَ u.i. حَسَدٌ envy.

أَذِنَ إِذْنٌ permit.

بَدَأَ a. بَدْءٌ and VIII begin.

امن IV believe.

اجر X hire, rent.

اثر V receive a mark, be influenced.

غنى X be self-sufficient.

لهو IV distract attention.

كفى i. كِفَايَةٌ be sufficient for.

شرى VIII buy.

بقى بَقَاءٌ remain.

نهى VIII let oneself be forbidden, desist.

ادب II educate.

أَمِنَ أَمَانٌ be safe from.

أَجَرَ u.i. أَجْرٌ hire out.

اثر II make a mark on, influence.

مَوْتٌ death.

جَمَالٌ beauty.

نَزَعَ i. نَزْعٌ take away.

عَرَفَ i. مَعْرِفَةٌ know.

الف II compose (a book), unite (men), win over.

هنأ II congratulate.

انس III treat kindly.

اخر II make late.

— V be late.

مَلَاكٌ ـ مَلَكٌ (مَلَائِكَةٌ) angel.

جِسْمٌ (a) body.

آخِرٌ last.

نَصِيبٌ share.

ولى II make one governor.

فقر VIII be poor, in need.

جاء i. جَيْءٌ come.

رَكَضَ u. رَكْضٌ run.

مَعْرُوفٌ known, kind act.

قل IV make little, support

مُعَمَّمٌ wearing a turban.

اثر IV prefer.

سَأَلَ a. سُؤَالٌ ask, beg.

نبأ IV tell.

كفأ III reward.

أَنِسَ أَنَسٌ be friendly.

جَدٌّ (a) grandfather.

عَمٌّ (a) paternal uncle.

عَمَّةٌ paternal aunt.

مَطَرٌ rain.

جار u. جَوَازٌ be allowable.

طَرَحَ a. طَرْحٌ throw down.

رسل III write letters to.

زَعَمَ a. زَعْمٌ think, claim.

رَغِبَ . رَغْبٌ في like, be pleased with ; عَنْ dislike.

زَرَعَ a. زَرْعٌ sow.

دَاءٌ (a) disease.

عِلْمٌ (b) knowledge, science.

سَرِيرٌ (أَسِرَّةٌ) anything on which one can sit or lie.

خَاتَمٌ (خَوَاتِمُ) seal.

وَصِيَّةٌ (وَصَايَا) will, testament.

تُهْمَةٌ suspicion.

وَعَى i. وَعْيٌ contain, understand.

عيى IV fatigue, distress.

وقى VIII be on one's guard, fear, be pious.

ودع II say good-bye.

وصى IV make a will, give a dying charge.

شاء a. مَشِيئَةٌ wish, will.

عَيِيَ a. عِيٌّ be weary.

وَقَى i. وِقَايَةٌ guard.

عفا u. عَفْوٌ pardon, refrain ; be abundant.

بَدَنٌ (a) body.

ذِهْنٌ mind, intellect.

جوز III pass beyond.

قَسَمَ i. قَسْمٌ divide.

رسل IV send.

وجع i. وَجَعٌ feel pain.

حَصَدَ u. حَصَادٌ reap.

دَوَاءٌ (أَدْوِيَةٌ) medicine, remedy.

أَدَبٌ (a) manners, arts.

صِحَّةٌ health.

ذَكَاءٌ sharpness (metaphorical).

صَحِيحٌ healthy, true.

ودع IV deposit.

نَفَعَ a. نَفْعٌ be useful to.

وهم VIII suspect.

حَلْيٌ (حُلِيٌّ) jewels.

أَبَدًا (with a negative) never.

سَهْمٌ (c) arrow, share.

سَمَكٌ (sing. سَمَكَةٌ) fish.

نَجَزَ u. نَجْزٌ finish off, fulfil.

وَدَعَ a. وَدْعٌ leave.

حيى II greet.

كرم IV honour.

حِلْمٌ statecraft, clemency, kindness.

قَدْرٌ amount, measure.

حَدِيثٌ (أَحَادِيثُ) story, report.

عَلِمَ عِلْمٌ know.

فَقْرٌ poverty.

حِرْصٌ greed.

أَسَدٌ (b) lion.

حُسْنٌ goodness, beauty.

سَمَاءٌ (سَمَوَاتٌ) sky, heaven.

شَيْءٌ (أَشْيَاءُ no nunation) thing.

قَوْمٌ (a) people, tribe, some.

فَزِعَ (فَزَعٌ) be afraid, seek refuge.

قَصَدَ i. قَصْدٌ aim at, purpose.

هَرَبَ u. هَرَبٌ run away.

شُغْلٌ (a) work, labour.

غَزَا u. غَزْوٌ raid, go to war.

بَكَى i. بُكَاءٌ weep.

نَهَى a. نَهْيٌ forbid.

وَلِيَ i. وَلْيٌ be near.

— IV do a kindness.

أَخَذَ u. أَخْذٌ take.

نَسِيَ نِسْيَانٌ forget.

جَنَى i. جَنْيٌ gather, جِنَايَةٌ commit a crime.

هَجَا . هِجَاءٌ lampoon.

غنى IV make rich, self-sufficient.

لَهَا u. لَهْوٌ play.

خَبَرٌ (a) story, news.

قَنِعَ قَنَاعَةٌ be content, satisfied.

بَلَاءٌ trial, misfortune.

شَرَهٌ greed.

حَرٌّ heat.

تَدْبِيرٌ management.

خُلْقٌ (a) nature, character.

أَحَدٌ fem. إِحْدَى one.

وَقْتٌ (a) time.

كَفٌّ restraint.

وَرَعٌ piety.

حَزِنَ حَزَنٌ be sorry.

رَحِمَ رَحْمَةٌ have mercy on.

خَوْفٌ fear.

اخذ VIII make, choose.

عِمَامَةٌ (عَمَائِمُ) turban.

قِلَادَةٌ (قَلَائِدُ) necklace.

عَصَبَ i. عَصْبٌ fold, tie.

حصى IV count.

حوط IV surround.

فقر IV make poor.

بغض IV hate, dislike.

حق X deserve.

قَلَّ i. قِلٌّ be little.

—X think little, be independent.

سَيِّدٌ (سَادَاتٌ سَادَةٌ) prince, chief.

حرك II move (trans.).

عاد u. عَوْدٌ return, do again.

شَتَمَ u. i. شَتْمٌ abuse.

نَشِبَ نَشْبٌ be attached to.

سَرُعَ سُرْعَةٌ be quick.

بَعُدَ بُعْدٌ be far, distant.

مَشْهُورٌ well known, famous.

فِرَاشٌ (d) bedding, furniture (i.e. cushions and rugs).

أَهْلٌ (أَهَالٍ) family.

ودع II say good-bye.

وكل II appoint as agent.

— VIII rely on.

وفق VIII agree.

حَالٌ f. (a) condition.

سَكَتَ u. سُكُوتٌ be quiet.

شُجَاعٌ bold.

سَمٌّ (b) poison

سَقَطَ u. سُقُوطٌ fall.

بَدْوٌ bedouins, nomads.

هَلَكَ i. هَلْكٌ perish.

هَلِكَ perish.

عَجِلَ عَجَلٌ hurry.

صَبَرَ i. صَبْرٌ be patient, endure.

ذَبَحَ a. ذَبْحٌ cut the throat, sacrifice.

فَقِهَ فِقْهٌ understand.

عَكَسَ i. عَكْسٌ turn upside down.

حَسُنَ حُسْنٌ be good.

حُكُومَةٌ government.

ضَيْعَةٌ (c) estate, village.

قُوتٌ (a) food.

أَمَةٌ (إِمَاءٌ) slave girl.

فِكْرٌ (a) thought, idea.

مَعْذِرَةٌ excuse.

مَفْجَرَةٌ sin (of any sort).

سَيِّءٌ bad.

كَرِهَ كُرْهٌ be unwilling, not like.

عَيْبٌ (b) fault, defect.

مَرِيضٌ (مَرْضَى) ill, sick.

فَرِيسَةٌ prey.

سَلِمَ سَلَامٌ be safe.

شَجَاعَةٌ bravery.

حَطَبٌ firewood.

ظَهَرَ a. ظُهُورٌ be manifest, conquer.

بَدَوِيٌّ a nomad.

سَفَرٌ (a) journey.

نَصِيحَةٌ advice, help.

حرك V move (intrans.).

هٰهُنَا — هُنَا here.

ثَمَّ there.

زاد i. زِيَادَةٌ increase (trans and intrans.).

لَبِثَ لَبْثٌ remain, stay.

صُبْحٌ (a) morning.

صبح II attack in the morning.

مَسَاءٌ evening.

حَصَلَ u. حُصُولٌ come to, befall (not of motion).

— II obtain.

رَزَقَ u. رِزْقٌ provide.

طِفْلٌ (a) infant.

عَظِيمٌ glorious, great.

أَمْرٌ (b) thing, affair.

سَهْلٌ level, easy.

قَتَلَ u. قَتْلٌ kill.

خَدَمَ i.u. خِدْمَةٌ serve.

مَنْزِلٌ — مَنْزِلَةٌ (مَنَازِلُ) house, camp, stage (of a journey).

غُلَامٌ (غِلْمَانٌ) young man, servant, boy.

عذب II punish.

صبح VIII drink in the morning.

غَدٌ next day.

غَدًا to-morrow.

رِزْقٌ (a) daily food, rations.

أُسْوَةٌ (إِسًا) model.

هُنَالِكَ — هُنَاكَ there.

حِينَئِذٍ then.

اَلْبَصْرَةُ Basra.

سفر III journey, travel.

سرع IV make quick, go fast.

بعد II, IV make distant.

علج III treat (illness, etc.).

عكس III oppose.

حسن IV make good, do well.

صَبَاحٌ morning.

أَنْفٌ (b) nose.

جُبْنٌ cheese.

سِرٌّ (a) secret.

أَمِينٌ faithful.

أَمْرٌ (أَوَامِرُ) command.

شَرَفٌ honour, nobility.

كَتَمَ u. كِتْمَانٌ hide (trans.)

ضَيْفٌ (a) guest.

عَذَابٌ punishment.

خَدٌّ (b) cheek.

جَبْهَةٌ (c) forehead.

سَكَنَ u. سُكُونٌ be quiet, dwell.

سَجَدَ u. سُجُودٌ bow down.

فَخَرَ u. فَخْرٌ boast.

مَكَثَ u. مَكْثٌ stay, remain.

غَرَسَ i. غَرْسٌ plant.

حَرِيرٌ silk.

مَرَّةٌ (c) time (repetition).

يَوْمٌ (أَيَّامٌ) day (24 hours).

لَيْلَةٌ one night.

مَكَانٌ (أَمْكِنَةٌ) place.

كِيسٌ (a) bag, purse.

سَاعَةٌ (سَاعَاتٌ) hour, moment.

كُفْرَانٌ be ungrateful.

دَمٌ (دِمَاءٌ) blood.

زَوْجٌ (a) pair, husband.

حَقٌّ (b) truth, duty, right.

رَسُولٌ (d) messenger, apostle.

صَفَحَ u. صَفْحٌ pardon.

عَقَدَ i. عَقْدٌ tie, knot.

كَبُرَ كِبَرٌ be big.

خَطَبَ u. خُطْبَةٌ preach, خِطَابٌ ask a woman in marriage.

طَلَقَ u. طَلَاقٌ be divorced.

عَتَبَ u. i. عَتْبٌ blame.

كَفَرَ u. كُفْرٌ be an unbeliever;

رَكِبَ رُكُوبٌ ride.

زَهَرَ a. زُهُورٌ bloom, shine.

قَعَدَ u. قُعُودٌ sit, stay at home.

غَرَبَ u. غُرُوبٌ be, go far off set (star).

صُوفٌ wool.

جُبْنٌ cowardice.

سَوْطٌ (a) whip.

لَيْلٌ (لَيَالٍ) night.

خَشْيَةٌ fear.

كُرْسِيٌّ (كَرَاسِيُّ) chair.

اَلْبَارِحُ yesterday.

رَبٌّ (a) lord.

زَوْجَةٌ wife.

إِنَّمَا only (adv.).

خَلَطَ i. خَلْطٌ mix.

حُمَّ (passive), suffer from fever.

حَمَّ u. حَمٌّ be hot.

حُمَّى fever.

فَاقَ u. فَوْقٌ be superior to.

عقد VIII believe.

كبر V be proud, act proudly.

IV divorce.

III blame, speak contemptuously

فِتْنَةٌ (فِتَنٌ) temptation, civil war.

خَرَقَ u. خَرْقٌ tear rend.

جرب II test.

بَرَدَ u. بَرْدٌ file.

عَبَرَ u. عُبورٌ pass over, cross.

تَعِبَ تَعَبٌ be tired.

تَعْبَانُ tired.

مَشْرِقٌ east, sunrise.

قَطُّ (with negative) ever.

شَيْطانٌ devil.

دَقَّ u. دَقٌّ hit, pound.

شهر VIII be well known.

زول IV remove.

سَهِرَ سَهَرٌ be wakeful at night.

أرخ II date.

تَأْرِيخٌ history.

ثَارَ u. ثَوْرٌ be stirred up.

شرك IV associate with (trans.).

لَزِمَ لُزُومٌ and VIII be attached to, be necessary.

دَفَنَ i. دَفْنٌ bury.

دَعَا دُعَاءٌ and X call, summon.

دَنَا دُنُوٌّ be near.

مَضَى مُضِيٌّ go, be past.

عَدَا عَدْوٌ go, go against.

عَقَبَ u. عَقْبٌ come after.

مَعْبَرٌ ferry.

مَخَاضٌ ford.

مَسْمَعٌ place from which is heard, ear.

مَأْمَنَةٌ place of safety.

مَبْعَثٌ time of sending, mission.

مُنْخُلٌ sieve.

مَسْأَلَةٌ question, problem.

غَسَلَ i. غَسْلٌ wash.

مَأْسَدَةٌ place where lions are plentiful.

مَغْرِبٌ west, sunset.

جَمِيعٌ (collected) together, all.

نظف II clean.

IV stir up.

VIII be associated with.

أَلِمَ أَلَمٌ suffer pain.

قلد II put a necklace on, invest with.

سر III whisper

وفى III arrive.

IV execute (order, etc.).

طَرَدَ u. طَرْدٌ drive, drive away round up.

حَلَفَ i. حَلْفٌ swear.	كَشَفَ i. كَشْفٌ uncover, disclose.
مَسَحَ a. مَسْحٌ measure.	مَزْرَعَةٌ (مَزَارِعُ) field.
شَهِدَ شُهُودٌ be present at.	مَرَضٌ (a) illness.
نَدِمَ نَدَمٌ repent.	حَيَاةٌ life.
سوف II make future, postpone.	جوب III, IV answer.
صَادَ i. صَيْدٌ hunt, fish.	قَادَ i. lead.
رود IV wish, will.	خير II give a choice to.
بقى X preserve, keep alive.	شبه III resemble.
تَابَ u. تَوْبَةٌ repent.	X ask to repent.
سَلَكَ u. سُلُوكٌ go.	جلس III sit with.
فوض III be partners, discuss.	نَكَحَ i.a. نِكَاحٌ marry.
صَلَحَ u. صَلَاحٌ be good, serviceable.	III make peace with.
	عَبَأَ a. عَبَأ (with negative) ignore.
— IV repair, restore.	عَمَّ u. be general, concern many.
كَدَّ u. كَدٌّ work hard, persevere.	بِرٌّ goodness, filial piety.
يَسَرَ i. يُسْرٌ be easy, easy-going.	II make easy.
— IV become rich.	فَضْلٌ excellence, superiority.
قَمِيصٌ (قُمْصَانٌ) shirt.	بَيْتٌ (a) verse of poetry.
حَرِيصٌ eager, greedy	بطؤ IV make slow, do slowly.
خَطَأٌ خِطْءٌ sin.	IV make a mistake.
يقظ IV wake up (trans.).	X wake up (intrans.).
رَهَنَ a. رَهْنٌ give a pledge to:	III wager.
رَبِحَ رِبْحٌ make a profit, be profitable.	عَاقِبَةٌ consequence.
	نَوْعٌ (a) kind, sort.
عَادَةٌ (عَادَاتٌ) custom.	جِنَازَةٌ — جَنَازَةٌ (جَنَائِزُ) funeral.
وَزِيرٌ (وُزَرَاءُ) minister of state.	وِزَارَةٌ ministry.

عجل II hasten, do quickly.

تَمَّ i. تَمٌّ be complete, perfect.

حَدَثَ u. حُدُوثٌ be new, happen

— IV make new, produce.

شَمَلَ u. شَمْلاً and شَمِلَ be common to, concern; VIII surround, consist of (عَلَى).

عَمِلَ عَمَلَ do, make, be a governor.

بَدَلَ u. بَدْلٌ change, exchange.

قَصَرَ u. قُصُورٌ be inadequate.

خَلَا u. خَلَاءٌ be empty, pass away

شَكَلَ u. شَكْلٌ and IV be involved, difficult.

فَضَلَ u. فَضْلٌ be in excess.

حَدَاثَةٌ newness, youth.

عَهْدٌ (b) agreement, treaty, time, period.

نُورٌ (a) light.

ذَخِيرَةٌ stores, treasure.

وَلْوَلَ wail.

ثَعْلَبٌ fox.

طَبِيعَةٌ nature.

جَنْبٌ (b) side.

وَثَاقٌ bonds.

مَيِّتٌ dead.

فَتَاةٌ (فَتَيَاتٌ) young woman.

II, IV complete.

شَكَّ u. شَكٌّ doubt.

صغر II make little.

حدث II tell.

حدث V, VI talk, converse.

زَلْزَلَةٌ earthquake.

X appoint, use.

عَمَلٌ (a) work, list.

مِنْشَفَةٌ towel.

هَضَمَ i. هَضْمٌ digest.

II make empty, leave.

مَلَكَ i. مُلْكٌ possess, be king.

نشف II make dry.

فَضِلَ u. be excellent.

دَهْرٌ epoch, age, time,

صَحْرَاءُ (صَحَارٍ) desert.

عَامِلٌ workman, governor.

خَلْوَةٌ private place, privacy.

قَدَرٌ God's decree, providence.

هَمٌّ (b) care, anxiety.

حَرَكَةٌ movement, vowel.

مَحْكَمَةٌ law court.

بَطِّيخٌ water melon.

حَيٌّ alive.

زَلْزَلَ shake (trans.).

عَمَدَ i. عَمْدٌ support, direct oneself towards.

شِرْكٌ polytheism.

دِيكٌ (b) cock.

عُمْرٌ (a) life, age.

خَفِيَ خَفَاءٌ be hidden.

فتى IV give counsel's opinion.

سَبَقَ u. سَبْقٌ precede, come in first.

ظَلَمَ i. ظُلْمٌ do wrong.

قَسَا قَسْوٌ be hard.

همّ VIII pay attention to, think important.

حَسَبَ u. حِسَابٌ count

حَضَرَ u. حُضُورٌ be present.

جَرَى i. جَرَيَانٌ run, flow.

زَهِدَ زُهْدٌ leave, be content with little, be ascetic.

شَهَا شَهْوَةٌ and VIII desire.

نَجَا نَجَاةٌ be safe, escape.

غنى IV make rich and independent, enable one to dispense with; (with negative) be useless in the face of.

عَصَى عِصْيَانٌ disobey.

دَجَاجٌ (دَجَاجَاتٌ) fowls, hens.

بِضَاعَةٌ (بَضَائِعُ) goods, merchandise.

عَنَى عَنَايَةٌ mean.

فَتْوَى counsel's opinion.

مَعْنًى meaning, idea.

شَكَا شَكْوَى complain.

III race.

صلو II say the ritual prayers.

IV be dark.

III find hard, oppressive.

بيض II whiten.

جَلَبَ u. جَلْبٌ come, bring, drive.

دِيوَانٌ (دَوَاوِينُ) ministry of state, register, collected works of a poet.

دَخْلٌ revenue.

حَسِبَ i. حِسْبَانٌ think.

جَادَ u. جُودَةٌ be generous.

حَذِرَ حَذَرٌ be on one's guard, be cautious.

قدر II estimate, imagine.

عزو II console, condole.

نَقَصَ u. نُقْصَانٌ be diminished, imperfect.

جَوَادٌ liberal; swift horse.

بين II explain.

رِيَ رَوِيَ be satisfied with drink.

عَذَرَ i. عُذْرٌ excuse, accept an excuse.

نَصِيرٌ helper.

عَطْشَانُ thirsty.

رَائِحَةٌ scent.

عُرْيَانٌ naked.

قَضَى قَضَاءٌ judge, settle, finish.

بَرَأَ بَرِئَ بُرُوٌّ بُرْءٌ be cured.

قرض IV lend.

خَلَصَ u. خُلُوصٌ be pure.

قلب II turn (trans.).

هَدَى هُدًى lead aright.

شَدَّ u. شِدَّةٌ attack, tie.

عسر IV be poor.

عَظُمَ عِظَمٌ be big.

حَقَرَ i. حَقْرٌ and VIII despise.

برك III (with على) bless.

كَسَبَ i. كَسْبٌ and VIII earn, earn a living.

عَجَزَ i. عَجْزٌ be weak, unable.

عَجِبَ عَجَبٌ and V wonder.

فَرَغَ u.a. فَرِغَ فُرُوغٌ be empty.

عَدِمَ عَدَمٌ be without, not to have.

امر VIII consult together.

حُرٌّ freeborn.

VIII excuse oneself.

مَوْلًى master, servant, freedman, cousin.

غَلِيظٌ rough, difficult.

أَحْمَقُ foolish.

فُرْصَةٌ opportunity.

زَمِنَ زَمَنٌ be paralysed.

II cure, acquit.

X ask a loan.

II make pure, save.

جَاعَ u. جُوعٌ be hungry.

لَطَفَ u. لُطْفٌ be kind.

نقم VIII punish.

طَأْطَأَ bow (the head).

II honour.

بَرَكَةٌ blessing.

هَدِيَّةٌ (هَدَايَا) gift.

حُمْقٌ folly.

عَطِشَ عَطَشٌ thirst.

IV weaken, incapacitate.

IV please.

II empty.

غَفَلَ u. غُفُولٌ neglect.

شَمَّ u. شَمٌّ smell.

زِرَاعَةٌ agriculture.

زَمَانٌ (أَزْمِنَةٌ) time, period.

دُعَاءٌ (أَدْعِيَةٌ) prayer, petition.

فَجْرٌ dawn.

غدو V eat the morning meal.

نَفَقَةٌ expenditure.

صِنَاعَةٌ handicraft, skill.

خَلَقٌ old, worn out.

صِنْفٌ (a) equal.

قُطْنٌ cotton.

عَارٌ defect, disgrace.

عِشَاءٌ evening.

عشو V eat the evening meal.

فَطَرَ u.i. فِطْرٌ break one's fast.

حَلِيفٌ ally.

قِدْرٌ (fem.) (b) cooking pot.

مَحَبَّةٌ love.

خَرْجٌ expenditure.

TRANSLATION

I shall not come in and not go away until you ride to
the mosque — either I go to Syria, and how unpleasant
that will be, or I stay ; and therein is a reward for me — we
claim that men are graded in excellence not by their fathers
but by their acts, their characters, their magnanimity, and
their high ambitions — the Arabs say of one who is asked
to give and cannot and refuses, my house is stingy not I
— I was alone with her and the moon showed her to me ;
when it disappeared she showed it to me — do not speak
of what you do not know lest you be suspected in what
you do know — do not forbid a quality (mode of behaviour)
and come to (do) something like it — the Arabs will not
consent to put you in authority as you are not one of them
— this poem is something which happened in youth ;
I made it about my wife. I was inclined to (in love with)
her, she was my slave and ruled my heart ; but now, I have
had no truck with such things for years and have not made
poetry for a long time.

لَا أَدْخُلُ وَلَا أَنْصَرِفُ أَوْ تَرْكَبَ إِلَى الْمَسْجِدِ ـ إِمَّا

أَنَا أَسِيرُ إِلَى الشَّأْمِ فَمَا أَكْرَهَهُ وَإِمَّا أَنْ أُقِيمَ فَلِي

فِيهِ أَجْرٌ ـ نَزْعُمُ أَنَّ تَفَاضُلَ النَّاسِ فِيمَا بَيْنَهُمْ لَيْسَ

بِآبَائِهِمْ وَلَكِنَّهُ بِأَفْعَالِهِمْ وَأَخْلَاقِهِمْ وَشَرَفِ نَفْسِهِمْ

وَبُعْدِ هِمَمِهِمْ ـ تَقُولُ الْعَرَبُ لِمَنْ سُئِلَ وَهُوَ لَا يَقْدِرُ

فَرَدَّ بَيْتِي يَبْخُلُ لَا أَنَا ـ خَلَوْتُ بِهَا وَالْقَمَرُ يُرِيهَا

فَلَمَّا غَابَ أَرْتَنِيهِ ـ لَا تَقُلْ فِيمَا لَا تَعْلَمُ فَتُتَّهَمَ فِيمَا تَعْلَمُ ـ لَا تَنْهَ عَنْ خُلُقٍ وَتَأْتِيَ مِثْلَهُ ـ لَا تَرْضَى اَلْعَرَبُ أَنْ يَسْتَعْمِلُوكَ وَأَنْتَ مِنْ غَيْرِهِمْ ـ هٰذَا اَلشِّعْرُ شَيْءٌ كَانَ فِي اَلْحَدَاثَةِ قُلْتُهُ فِي زَوْجَتِي وَكُنْتُ إِلَيْهَا مَائِلًا وَكَانَتْ لِي مَمْلُوكَةً وَلِقَلْبِي مَالِكَةً فَأَمَّا اَلْآنَ فَلَا عَهْدَ لِي بِمِثْلِهِ مُنْذُ سِنِينَ وَلَا عَمِلْتُ شِعْرًا مُنْذُ دَهْرٍ طَوِيلٍ .

he told them to bring their books — what do you think of Egypt ? — these women, will they perform what they have promised ? — be on your guard against suspicion — they greeted [illegible] politely — show me how that will benefit me — ask the keeper to show you what the boxes contain — fear God and honour the king — I prefer that men should fear me than that they should fear God — bring me my share of the food and I will eat it by the river — did you not all see what your aunt wrote ? — much study wearies the young.

أَمَرَهُمْ أَنْ يَأْتُوا بِكُتُبِهِمْ ـ كَيْفَ رَأَيْتَ مِصْرَ ـ هٰؤُلَاءِ اَلنِّسَاءُ هَلْ تَفِينَ مَا وَعَدْنَ ـ اِتَّقُوا اَلْاِتِّهَامَ ـ حَيَّوْنَا تَحِيَّةَ اَلْكَرِيمِ ـ أَرِنِي كَيْفَ ذٰلِكَ يَنْفَعُنِي ـ

سَلِ ٱلْحَافِظَ أَنْ يُرِيَكَ مَا فِى ٱلصَّنَادِيقِ ـ اِتَّقُوا
ٱللّٰهَ وَأَكْرِمُوا ٱلْمَلِكَ ـ أُوثِرُ أَنْ يَخَافَنِى ٱلنَّاسُ مِنْ
أَنْ يَتَّقُوا ٱللّٰهَ ـ اِيتِنِى سَهْمِى مِنَ ٱلطَّعَامِ فَآكُلَهُ
عِنْدَ ٱلنَّهْرِ ـ أَلَمْ تَرَوْا كُلُّكُمْ مَا كَتَبَتْ عَمَّتُكُمْ ـ
إِنَّ ٱلدَّرْسَ ٱلْكَثِيرَ يُعْيِى ٱلصِّغَارَ.

his name is famous in the east and the west — the thief came in like a lion and went out like a sheep — all his children swim like fish — as long as life remains I shall not leave the battle field — the child cut off his finger with the tailor's scissors — he washes his dog twice daily — reason is to a man a file with which he files the roughness of the heart, a broom with which he removes evil deeds. a mallet with which he bruises the head of the devil, and a sieve with which he cleans his thoughts — the Syrian boasts of the snow and fruits of his mountains and the Egyptian of the water of his river — the carpenter must not be ignorant of the qualities of the different kinds of wood.

اِشْتَهَرَ ٱسْمُهُ فِى ٱلْمَشْرِقِ وَٱلْمَغْرِبِ ـ دَخَلَ ٱللِّصُّ
دِخْلَةَ ٱلْأَسَدِ وَخَرَجَ خِرْجَةَ ٱلشَّاةِ ـ يَسْبَحُ أَوْلَادُهُ
جَمِيعًا سِبْحَةَ ٱلسَّمَكِ ـ مَا دَامَتِ ٱلْحَيَاةُ لَا أَتْرُكُ
ٱلْمُقَاتَلَ ـ قَطَعَ ٱلطِّفْلُ إِصْبَعَهُ بِمِقَصِّ ٱلْخَيَّاطِ ـ يَغْسِلُ

كَلْبَهُ كُلَّ يَوْمٍ غَسْلَتَيْنِ ـ إِنَّ ٱلْعَقْلَ لِلْإِنْسَانِ مِبْرَدٌ
يَبْرُدُ بِهِ خُشُونَةَ ٱلْقَلْبِ وَمِكْنَسَةٌ يُزِيلُ بِهَا أَعْمَالَ
ٱلسُّوْءِ وَمِدَقٌّ يَدُقُّ بِهِ رَأْسَ ٱلشَّيْطَانِ وَمُنْخُلٌ يُنَظِّفُ
بِهِ أَفْكَارَهُ ـ يَفْتَخِرُ ٱلشَّامِيُّ بِثَلْجِ جِبَالِهِ وَفَوَاكِهِهَا
وَٱلْمِصْرِيُّ بِمَاءِ نَهْرِهِ ـ مَا كَانَ لِلنَّجَّارِ أَنْ يَجْهَلَ
كَيْفِيَّاتِ أَنْوَاعِ ٱلْخَشَبِ ٱلْمُخْتَلِفَةِ .

he sat like a tired man — have you ever h[illegible] the like of this? he said, no, the like of it has never torn my ears — Moses hit the stone once and water came out enough for all the people — the woman of the house drove out the thief, hitting him with the broom — cause them to hear the word of God and bring them to their place of safety — we journeyed some stages and reached a place where lions were numerous where we feared for our horses — let us now mention the history from the birth of the apostle of God to (the time of) his mission — they tried me with questions of which I understood nothing — we crossed the river, some by a ferry and some by a ford — he was the most remembering of men for what he heard, the least of them in (need of) sleep, and the most enduring of wakefulness.

جَلَسَ جِلْسَةَ ٱلتَّعْبَانِ ـ أَسَمِعْتَ مِثْلَ هٰذَا قَطُّ قَالَ لَا مَا
خَرَقَ مَسَامِعِي قَطُّ مِثْلُهُ ـ ضَرَبَ مُوسَى ٱلْحَجَرَ ضَرْبَةً

وَيَخْرُجُ مَاءٌ يَكْفِي ٱلْقَوْمَ جَمِيعًا ـ أَخْرَجَتْ صَاحِبَةُ ٱلْبَيْتِ ٱللِّصَّ تَضْرِبُهُ بِٱلْمِكْنَسَةِ ـ أَسْمِعُوهُمْ كَلَامَ ٱللهِ وَأَبْلِغُوهُمْ مَأْمَنَهُمْ ـ سَافَرْنَا مَنَازِلَ وَبَلَغْنَا مَأْسَدَةً نَخَافُ فِيهَا عَلَى خَيْلِنَا ـ فَلْنَذْكُرِ ٱلْآنَ ٱلتَّأْرِيخَ مِنْ مَوْلِدِ رَسُولِ ٱللهِ إِلَى مَبْعَثِهِ ـ جَرَّبُونِي بِمَسَائِلَ لَمْ أَفْهَمْ مِنْهَا شَيْئًا ـ عَبَرْنَا ٱلنَّهْرَ بَعْضُنَا فِي مَعْبَرٍ وَبَعْضُنَا بِمَخَاضَةٍ ـ كَانَ أَحْفَظَ ٱلنَّاسِ لِمَا سَمِعَ وَأَقَلَّهُمْ نَوْمًا وَأَصْبَرَهُمْ عَلَى ٱلسَّهَرِ .